Dean Edwards
MINCESPIRATION!

Dean Edwards
MINCESPIRATION!

Over 100 budget-friendly, quick
and easy family meals with mince

BANTAM PRESS

LONDON · TORONTO · SYDNEY · AUCKLAND · JOHANNESBURG

TRANSWORLD PUBLISHERS
61–63 Uxbridge Road, London W5 5SA
A Random House Group Company
www.transworldbooks.co.uk

First published in Great Britain
in 2013 by Bantam Press
an imprint of Transworld Publishers

A CIP catalogue record for this book
is available from the British Library.

ISBN 9780593070864

Addresses for Random House Group Ltd companies outside the UK
can be found at: www.randomhouse.co.uk
The Random House Group Ltd Reg. No. 954009

The Random House Group Limited supports the Forest Stewardship Council (FSC®), the
leading international forest-certification organization. Our books carrying the FSC label are
printed on FSC®-certified paper. FSC is the only forest-certification scheme endorsed by
the leading environmental organizations, including Greenpeace. Our paper procurement
policy can be found at www.randomhouse.co.uk/environment.

Photography: Martin Poole
Design & art direction: Smith & Gilmour
Editorial: Jinny Johnson
Food styling: Aya Nishimura
Props styling: Tamzin Ferdinando
Proof reading: Elise See Tai

CONTENTS

MARVELLOUS MINCE

You may be wondering why I've chosen to dedicate such a large chunk of my life to an ingredient as humble as mince? The reason is simple – passion! I know we hear the P word in every other sentence on television cookery shows, no more so than on *Masterchef*, where I started my journey in the professional world of food, but I mean it. So many fantastic dishes can be created from ordinary minced beef, lamb, pork, chicken or turkey. You might not often find mince on the menus of high-end restaurants, but it does appear on family dinner tables up and down the country every day, and it's one of the most useful ingredients we have in the kitchen.

Like so many people, I grew up eating mince. When I started to think of mince-inspired meals, I quickly realized that the boundaries for inspiration were limitless, hence the title of this book – *Mincespiration*. I've discovered that every cuisine has ways of making delicious food with economical minced meat. For example, my South African nan used to cook an amazing Malay mince and pea curry – I can still taste it now. It was packed with flavour and, best of all, it would feed the whole family with minimum impact on the shopping budget.

In fact, one of the many great things about mince is its price. You can make hearty meals that will go a long way for a small outlay. This also made mince the perfect subject for my first cookbook, as my friends call me 'the fork' and not for cooking reasons. Apparently it's because I'm tight with money. One friend says that I'm so tight that when he came round for a cup of tea I'd put a fork in the sugar bowl to make it go further!

When I was a child, I used to love watching my dad mincing meat at home to use in a lasagne or curry. For a relatively small sum, you can buy your own mincer and grind up pretty much anything from pork belly for adding fat and flavour to a burger, to more exotic meats such as game and venison. Nowadays, though, most of us buy our minced meat from the supermarket or local butcher. A 500g pack of beef mince can cost as little as £2.50, so I reckon a great many of these dishes will suit even the tightest of budgets, while still delighting the taste buds. As always, the better the meat the better the dish and I recommend buying the best you can afford for top results. Mince also freezes well so take the opportunity to stock up and you'll always have the ingredients for a good meal to hand.

As well as using mince, try removing sausages from their skins and, with the help of herbs and spices, transforming the meat into amazing dishes such as an Asian-inspired tom yum soup. Or how about turning chorizo sausage into a fiery topping for a carnivore's adaptation of Spanish patatas bravas?

I love every one of the recipes in this book, but feel free to switch and swap ingredients to suit your tastes and diet requirements. I believe that some of the best home-cooked meals start with a basic recipe that gradually evolves as you add a few tweaks here and there and make it your own. These are the sorts of recipes that you end up cooking for your family for years to come. Mince is inexpensive, versatile and, most important of all, delicious. Have fun!

USEFUL TIPS

Onions, garlic, shallots, potatoes and other vegetables should always be peeled before preparing, unless otherwise specified.

I always use medium eggs in my recipes, and I generally prefer to cook with free-range eggs, but this is up to you. I have specified free-range in recipes where eggs are the stars of the show, such as my beef hash with poached eggs.

I usually use olive oil in my cooking and vegetable oil for deep-frying, but go with your personal preference.

Chillies can vary a great deal in heat and everyone's tolerance to them varies as well. In some recipes I've suggested deseeding the chillies, but again it's up to you.

Lemon grass is becoming much more familiar and is easy to find in supermarkets and greengrocers. Don't be put off – it's easy to prepare. Simply give a good bash with a rolling pin before using it to release its fragrant oils.

I've tried to keep things as simple and straightforward as possible so you won't need lots of special equipment for making these recipes. A proper non-stick frying pan makes life much easier though, and a good-quality item will last for ages.

BROWNING MINCE

There really is no right or wrong way when it comes to browning mince, but here are a few pointers that might help. One question I'm often asked is whether or not to use oil. I've suggested adding a dash of oil when browning mince, but it really does depend on the quality of the meat. Most of the beef mince you buy in supermarkets and butchers will have a 20 per cent fat to meat ratio so you'll probably need a dash of oil to help start the frying process, but a fattier mince may need none at all.

I like to get my pan searing hot before adding the oil (if any) and mince. There is nothing worse than letting your mince stew away in its own juices. Avoid overcrowding the pan too, or the mince will stew rather than brown. I like to start to caramelize my mince so it's really lovely and brown, as I think this adds a greater depth of flavour to the finished dish.

You'll notice that in many of the recipes I say to chill the meatballs or burgers for 30 minutes before cooking them. This helps the fat set, so once you start cooking, there's less chance that the meatballs or burgers will break up and lose their shape. If you just don't have time, skip this step, but be gentle when cooking your mince.

CHAPTER 1
BEEF MINCE

Beef is the most familiar minced meat and probably the most popular. I grew up on it and still fondly recall the hearty meals of spaghetti bolognese and chilli con carne that my parents cooked on a regular basis. This chapter includes all the old favourites but also introduces you to some new, exciting dishes that I hope will become family standbys for years to come – recipes such as beef kofta curry (see p. 14), the ultimate blue cheese and jalapeño burgers (see p. 19), and my warming spicy minced beef cobbler (see p. 25).

When you are buying beef mince, always check the labels specifying the fat content. Standard mince should contain no more than 20 per cent fat and lean mince no more than 10 per cent fat. Look for the amount of white marbling of fat within the mince. I know that many of us are on a tight budget these days, but try to buy the best minced beef you can afford. For some recipes, such as burgers, I've specified lean steak mince for the best results.

I love Italian food. The dishes have such bold flavours but they're usually so simple to make. Oven-baked cannelloni is right up there for me as the ultimate comfort food. The only thing I ask is that you make the white sauce from scratch – no shop-bought tubs here! The sauce is very simple and once you get the hang of it you'll never use ready-made again. Making your own is much cheaper too. SERVES 4

BEEF AND MUSHROOM CANNELLONI

olive oil
300g mushrooms, wiped
    and sliced (chestnut and
    Portobello are both great)
400g beef mince
1 onion, finely chopped
3 garlic cloves, crushed
100ml white wine
200ml passata
4 sheets of fresh lasagne
    pasta
70g Parmesan cheese, grated
sea salt
black pepper

White sauce
40g unsalted butter
40g plain flour
400ml milk
small grating of nutmeg

1 Heat a dash of oil in a non-stick frying pan and fry the mushrooms until browned. Remove the mushrooms from the pan and set them aside.

2 Using the same pan, add a little more oil and fry the beef for 4–5 minutes until browned. Add the onion and garlic and continue cooking for 2–3 minutes. Pour in the wine and cook until the liquid is reduced by half, then pour in the passata and simmer for 5 minutes. Put the mushrooms back in the pan and season with salt and pepper.

3 To make the white sauce, melt the butter in a small saucepan over a medium heat, then whisk in the flour and cook for 1–2 minutes. With the pan on the heat, gradually pour in the milk and keep whisking until you have a smooth sauce. Turn down the heat, cook for 7–8 minutes, then season with salt, pepper and nutmeg.

4 Grease a baking dish measuring about 33 x 23cm. Preheat the oven to 200°C/180°C Fan/Gas 6. Lay a sheet of lasagne on a board, spoon on some filling, a little cheese and a dash of the white sauce. Roll up the lasagne sheet and place it in the dish. Repeat until you've used all the beef mixture, then pour over the remaining white sauce and sprinkle with the rest of the cheese. Bake in the oven for 30 minutes or until browned.

This kofta curry is a beauty. Dry-frying and grinding the whole spices will give you a much punchier taste, but use ground spices if you like. Bear in mind, though, that ground spices do go out of date and lose their flavour, so no using the spice rack given to you on your wedding day in 1982! Delicious served with rice and naan bread. SERVES 4

BEEF KOFTA CURRY

500g beef mince
1/2 onion, finely chopped
3 tbsp chopped fresh
   coriander, plus
   extra for serving
2 tsp garam masala
1–2 tsp chilli powder
   (or to taste)
olive oil
2 handfuls of baby spinach
sea salt
black pepper

Sauce
1 tsp coriander seeds
1 tsp cumin seeds
1 tsp mustard seeds
olive oil
1 1/2 onions, finely sliced
4 garlic cloves, crushed
1 thumb-sized piece of
   fresh root ginger, peeled
   and grated
1 tbsp garam masala
1/2 tsp turmeric
1/2 tsp cinnamon
500ml passata
1 x 400g can of coconut milk

1 First make the koftas. Put the mince, onion, 3 tablespoons of fresh coriander, garam masala and chilli powder into a bowl, season with salt and pepper and mix thoroughly. Shape the mixture into about 12 golf ball-sized balls. Heat a dash of oil in a non-stick frying pan and fry the koftas for about 5 minutes, until browned. Remove them from the pan and set aside.

2 For the sauce, dry-fry the coriander, cumin and mustard seeds in a small pan for 1 minute, then grind them in a pestle and mortar.

3 Add another dash of oil to the pan you used for frying the koftas and cook the sliced onions, garlic and ginger for about 10 minutes until softened. Add the freshly ground spices and the other spices and cook for a further 2–3 minutes. Pour in the passata and coconut milk, bring the mixture to a simmer, then put the koftas back in the pan. Cover and cook for 40–50 minutes over a gentle heat.

4 Just before the end of the cooking time, add the spinach and cook until wilted. Season and stir in the extra coriander just before serving.

Spaghetti bolognese, or pasta with beef ragù sauce, is now one of Britain's best-loved dishes, but the version many of us eat is far removed from the Italian classic. This is the recipe that I was brought up on and have grown to love, and even if I have to throw on some Cheddar instead of Parmesan it's still great! Definitely has to be served with garlic bread. SERVES 4

BEEF RAGÙ PASTA

olive oil
500g beef mince
2 onions, finely chopped
4 garlic cloves, crushed
100g smoked, cubed pancetta
300ml red wine
2 x 400g cans of chopped
   tomatoes
1 tbsp tomato purée
300ml beef stock
1 tbsp dried oregano
small pinch of sugar
300g spaghetti
small bunch of fresh basil,
   leaves torn
grated Parmesan cheese,
   for serving
sea salt
black pepper

1 Heat a large saucepan, add a dash of oil, then fry the mince for 5–6 minutes over a high heat until browned. Add the onions, garlic and pancetta and cook for another 6–7 minutes, then pour in the red wine. Continue to cook until the liquid has reduced by half.

2 Add the tomatoes, tomato purée, stock and oregano and mix well. Bring the sauce to a simmer, then cover and cook over a low heat for 1 1/2 hours – a long time I know, but well worth the wait! Season with salt, pepper and a small pinch of sugar.

3 Cook the pasta in plenty of salted boiling water according to the packet instructions, then drain. Toss it with the ragù sauce and fresh basil, then serve with grated Parmesan.

This rich, creamy Malaysian curry hits all the right notes. Traditionally it is made with the tougher cuts of beef, such as skirt steak, and cooked for a long time, but by using mince you can achieve the delicious flavour associated with a rendang in a fraction of the time. Serve with jasmine rice (see p. 199) and wedges of lime. SERVES 4

MALAYSIAN BEEF RENDANG

500g beef mince
50g desiccated coconut
olive oil
2 onions, diced
4 garlic cloves, crushed
1 thumb-sized piece of
   fresh root ginger, peeled
   and grated
1–2 large red chillies,
   deseeded and chopped
2 large sticks of lemon grass
1 tsp garam masala
1/2 tsp turmeric
1 tsp paprika
1 tsp cinnamon
1 tbsp brown sugar
1 x 400ml can of coconut milk
juice of 1/2 lime
2 shallots, finely sliced
1 tbsp chopped fresh
   coriander, for garnish
sea salt
black pepper

1 Season the mince with salt and pepper, then shape it into about 16 meatballs. Cover them with cling film and place in the fridge to chill while you prepare the rest of the dish.

2 Toast the coconut in a dry pan over a medium heat until just coloured. Remove the coconut from the pan and set aside.

3 Heat a dash of oil in a non-stick frying pan and fry the meatballs for 6–7 minutes. Add the onions, garlic, ginger and chillies and cook for another 5 minutes. Bruise the lemon grass by bashing it with a rolling pin to release the flavour and add it to the pan with the spices, toasted coconut and sugar. Pour in the coconut milk. Bring everything to the boil, then turn the heat to low and cook uncovered for 40–50 minutes. The sauce should be thick, rich and coating the meatballs. Season with salt and pepper and a squeeze of lime juice. Remove the lemon grass.

4 Meanwhile, heat another pan, add a dash of oil and fry the shallots over a medium to high heat until golden brown. Keep stirring them so they don't burn. To serve, sprinkle the crispy shallots over the rendang and garnish with freshly chopped coriander.

Burgers are a weakness of mine and this recipe combines all my favourite toppings in one burger. A good burger done properly is a thing of beauty so always try to use the best-quality beef you can afford. It really does make a difference when it comes to burgers. **SERVES 6**

BLUE CHEESE AND JALAPEÑO BURGERS

olive oil
1 small onion, finely chopped
700g lean steak mince
30g pickled jalapeño chillies, chopped
1/2 red onion, sliced into rings
30ml red wine vinegar
1/2 tsp sugar
12 thin slices of chorizo
150g Dolcelatte cheese, crumbled
6 burger buns
1 beef tomato, sliced
2 handfuls of watercress
sea salt
black pepper

1 Warm a dash of oil in a non-stick frying pan, add the onion and cook for 5–6 minutes until softened. Leave to cool. Combine the mince, cooled onion and jalapeños in a bowl and season with salt and plenty of black pepper. Divide the mixture into 6 burgers, then cover with cling film and place in the fridge to chill for 30 minutes.

2 Meanwhile, put the red onion slices in a small bowl with the vinegar and sugar and leave them to marinate for 5 minutes. Drain and set aside.

3 Heat a dry pan and cook the slices of chorizo for about 1 minute on each side until nice and crispy, then remove and set aside. Leave any oil from the chorizo in the pan as it will add flavour to the burger. Preheat the oven to 190°C/170°C Fan/Gas 5.

4 Cook the burgers for 5–6 minutes on each side in the hot pan, adding a touch more oil if needed. Transfer them to a baking tray and top with some chorizo slices and Dolcelatte. Pop the burgers into the preheated oven for a couple of minutes or until the cheese has melted. Toast the buns.

5 Serve the burgers on the toasted buns with some tomato slices, watercress and marinated red onions.

I call this the ultimate bad boy because it's big, juicy and tasty, just like every burger should be. I like to take my holidays in the States and make it my mission to find and eat the biggest and best burgers I can lay my hands on. This is my version, using a combination of pork and beef mince for great flavour. I often prepare double the amount and put some uncooked burgers in the freezer for another day. SERVES 4

THE ULTIMATE BAD BOY BURGER

250g lean steak mince
250g pork mince
2 shallots, finely diced
1 egg yolk
50g Parmesan cheese, grated
1 tbsp Worcester sauce
olive oil
60g mature Cheddar
   cheese, grated
4 burger buns
handful of watercress
6 cornichons, sliced
   lengthways
sea salt
black pepper

Slow-roasted tomatoes
6 ripe plum tomatoes, halved
20ml olive oil
1 tbsp balsamic vinegar
1 tsp sugar
2 garlic cloves, crushed

1 First prepare the tomatoes. Preheat the oven to 170°C/150°C Fan/Gas 3½. Place the tomato halves on a baking tray and drizzle them with the olive oil and balsamic vinegar, then sprinkle on the sugar and garlic. Roast for 45–50 minutes.

2 For the burgers, combine the minced steak and pork, shallots, egg yolk, Parmesan cheese and Worcester sauce in a bowl and season well with salt and pepper. Divide the mixture into 4 patties, then cover with cling film and chill them in the fridge for 30 minutes.

3 Preheat a griddle pan. Brush the burgers with a little oil and cook them for about 5–6 minutes on each side. Top with grated Cheddar, then place the burgers under a hot grill for a minute or so until the cheese has melted.

4 Toast the buns. Place the burgers on to the buns and top with some watercress, tomatoes and cornichons. Serve right away.

This is my carnivores' version of the Mexican classic known as *huevos rancheros*, which literally translated means 'ranch eggs'. Traditionally, this is a spicy breakfast dish used to kick-start a cowboy's day. However, my version makes a great family supper, best served with a portion of rice on the side. I sometimes grate a bit of Cheddar cheese over the top too and add a dollop of soured cream. SERVES 4

CHILLI BEEF MEXICAN EGGS

olive oil
500g beef mince
80g chorizo, cut into
   1cm cubes
1 onion, very finely diced
3 garlic cloves, crushed
1 tsp freshly ground cumin
   seeds
½ tsp ground cinnamon
1–2 tsp chilli powder
   (or more to taste)
1 tsp dried oregano
2 x 400g cans of chopped
   tomatoes
1 x 400g can of red kidney
   beans, drained and rinsed
150ml beef stock
4 free-range eggs
2 tbsp chopped fresh
   coriander, for serving
sea salt
black pepper

1 Heat a large non-stick pan (you need one that has a lid), add a dash of oil and brown the mince. Remove the browned mince from the pan and set it aside, then add the chorizo, onion and garlic to the pan and cook for 4–5 minutes. Add the cumin, cinnamon, chilli powder and oregano and cook for another 1–2 minutes.

2 Put the mince back in the pan and add the tomatoes, beans and stock. Bring to the boil, then cook over a medium heat for 15–20 minutes or until the mixture has slightly thickened. Season with salt and pepper towards the end of the cooking time.

3 Make 4 wells in the chilli beef mixture and crack an egg into each one. Cover the pan with a lid and cook the eggs for 8–10 minutes or until the whites have set. Garnish with some fresh coriander before serving.

Picture a cold winter's night with fireworks popping in the background and the smell of this cobbler cooking in the oven. Sounds perfect, so why not give it a go? I am a big fan of cobblers, both sweet and savoury, as they remind me so much of my childhood. Serve with some horseradish-spiked parsnip mash (see p. 195) – lovely. **SERVES 4**

SPICY MINCED BEEF COBBLER

olive oil
500g beef mince
80g smoked, cubed pancetta
1 onion, finely chopped
150g baby button mushrooms
2 carrots, diced
1 tbsp fresh thyme (leaves
   picked from the stems)
2 garlic cloves, crushed
150ml red wine
300ml beef stock
200ml passata
1 tbsp Worcester sauce
sea salt
black pepper

Cobbler topping
120g self-raising flour
50g unsalted butter, diced
1 tbsp fresh thyme (leaves
   picked from the stems)
pinch of salt
1 egg, beaten
1 tbsp horseradish sauce
3–4 tbsp milk
1 egg, beaten, for glazing
   the cobbler

1 Heat a dash of oil in a non-stick saucepan and brown the beef mince. Remove the mince from the pan and set it aside, then add the pancetta, onion, mushrooms, carrots, thyme and garlic and cook for 7–8 minutes or until softened.

2 Pour in the wine and continue to cook until the liquid is reduced by half, then add the stock, passata and Worcester sauce. Bring the mixture to a simmer, put the mince back in the pan and cook gently for 20 minutes. Season with salt and pepper.

3 To make the topping, sift the flour into a bowl and rub in the butter until the mixture resembles breadcrumbs. Add the thyme and salt, then stir in the beaten egg and horseradish. Add the milk, 1 tablespoon at a time, mixing until you have a thick batter. Preheat the oven to 180°C/160°C Fan/Gas 4.

4 Tip the meat mixture into an ovenproof dish measuring about 33 x 23cm. Dot 6–8 tablespoons of the batter on top, making sure the 'cobbles' don't touch so they have room to spread. Brush the top of the cobbler with beaten egg, then bake in the preheated oven for about 35 minutes or until golden.

When I was a kid, I used to love the beef tacos my dad sometimes knocked up for dinner. What I didn't love was getting absolutely covered in food as I tried to pick up and eat the fragile taco shells! This inspired me to create this dish, which draws on the same combination of flavours but is much easier to eat because these taco baskets are more robust. Serve with some rice if you like. SERVES 4

JALAPEÑO BEEF TACO BASKETS

olive oil
500g beef mince
1 onion, finely chopped
1 green pepper, diced
2 garlic cloves, chopped
1 tsp smoked paprika
1 tsp ground cumin
2 tbsp tomato purée
250ml beef stock
4 flour tortillas
1 jar of pickled jalapeños, drained
2 tbsp chopped fresh coriander
1/4 iceberg lettuce, shredded
sea salt
black pepper

1 Heat a non-stick frying pan, add a dash of oil and fry the beef for 4–5 minutes over a high heat. Add the onion, green pepper and garlic and cook for another 3–4 minutes. Stir in the spices, purée and stock, then simmer over a low to medium heat for 20–25 minutes. Season with salt and pepper.

2 While the meat is cooking, make the taco baskets. Preheat the oven to 160°C/140°C Fan/ Gas 3. Place each tortilla over an upside-down ovenproof bowl – something the size of a cereal bowl is fine – and bake in the preheated oven for 8–10 minutes, being careful not to brown the tortillas too much. Leave the tortillas to cool on the bowls, then place them on a serving plate.

3 Add a large spoonful of mince to each taco basket and top with some pickled jalapeños, fresh coriander and shredded lettuce. Serve at once.

Quesadillas are great for a quick lunchtime snack or as an evening meal the whole family will enjoy. Think of them as a Mexican sandwich and include any filling you like – throw in some sweetcorn, black beans or freshly chopped ripe tomatoes. Serve with some cooling guacamole (see p. 156) or fiery hot salsa. **SERVES 4**

MEXICAN BEEF QUESADILLAS

olive oil
300g beef mince
100g chorizo, diced
1 small red onion, finely
  chopped
1 tsp ground cumin
1 tsp smoked paprika
8 flour tortillas
250g Cheddar cheese,
  grated
1 green chilli, very finely diced
  (deseed if you prefer)
3 tbsp chopped fresh
  coriander
sea salt
black pepper

1 Heat a non-stick frying pan, add a dash of oil and fry the mince for 5–6 minutes until it is starting to brown. Add the chorizo, onion and spices and cook for a further 3–4 minutes, then season with salt and pepper.

2 Place a quarter of the mince mixture on top of a tortilla. Sprinkle over some cheese, chilli and coriander, then place another tortilla on top to make a sandwich. Make the remaining quesadillas in the same way.

3 Place a dry non-stick pan over a medium heat and fry the quesadillas, 1 at a time, for about 2 minutes on each side. Slice each quesadilla into 6 and serve immediately.

We are lucky enough to have a large Caribbean community in Bristol, with restaurants and stalls serving up such classics as curried goat and brown stew chicken. Perhaps the most famous dish of all is jerk chicken. Jerk was traditionally a way of preserving meat, but believe me this meal won't last long enough to need preserving! My twist takes the jerk spices and breathes life into an ordinary burger. Serve with the salsa, crusty rolls, watercress and a dollop of lime-spiked mayo (see p. 203). Amazing! SERVES 4

JERKED MINCE PATTIES

olive oil
1 onion, very finely chopped
2 garlic cloves, crushed
1 red chilli, finely diced
    (deseed if you prefer)
1 small piece of fresh root
    ginger, peeled and grated
500g beef mince
1 heaped tsp ground coriander
1 tsp ground allspice
1 tbsp fresh thyme (leaves
    picked from the stems)
small grating of nutmeg
1/2 tsp cinnamon
50g breadcrumbs
sea salt
black pepper

Mango salsa
1 mango, flesh diced
1/2 red onion, finely diced
1 tbsp chopped fresh
    coriander
1 tbsp chopped fresh mint
1/2 red chilli, finely diced
1 tsp grated fresh root ginger
juice of 1/2 lime
1 tbsp olive oil

1 Warm a dash of oil in a non-stick frying pan, add the onion, garlic, chilli and ginger and fry for about 5 minutes until softened. Leave to cool for 10 minutes.

2 Put the beef mince in a large bowl with the cooled onion mixture and the rest of the patty ingredients. Mix until thoroughly combined, then season with a good pinch of salt and pepper. Divide the mixture into 4, then shape the portions into burgers, cover with cling film and chill them in the fridge for 30 minutes.

3 Put the frying pan back on the heat and add a dash more oil. Fry the burgers over a medium heat for 5–7 minutes on each side or until they are cooked through.

4 To make the salsa, mix the diced mango with the onion, coriander, mint, chilli (deseeded if you prefer) and ginger, then stir well. Add the lime juice and olive oil, season with salt and pepper and serve with the burgers.

Spice up your mealtimes with these beautiful stuffed peppers, which are flavoured with garam masala, an Indian blend of spices. Every family has its closely guarded secret recipe for this mixture, which is passed down from generation to generation, but it generally includes cumin, coriander, cinnamon, cardamom and cloves. It's a spice I always keep in my store cupboard for adding depth of flavour to a home-made curry. **SERVES 4**

KEEMA ALOO STUFFED PEPPERS

1 large potato, diced into 1cm cubes
olive oil
400g beef mince
1 onion, sliced
1 small piece of fresh root ginger, peeled and finely chopped
2 garlic cloves, crushed
1 red chilli, deseeded and chopped
1 tbsp garam masala
1 tsp cumin
1/2 tsp turmeric
1/2 x 400g can of chopped tomatoes
200ml beef stock
1 tsp sugar
4 red peppers
1 tbsp chopped fresh coriander, to garnish
sea salt
black pepper

1 Put the potato cubes in a saucepan of salted water, bring to the boil and cook for 3 minutes. Drain and set aside.

2 Heat a non-stick frying pan, add a dash of oil and fry the beef mince over a very high heat for 8–10 minutes. Then add the onion, ginger, garlic, chilli and spices and continue cooking for 5 minutes. Add the tomatoes and potatoes to the pan and pour in just enough stock to cover. Cook for 13–15 minutes, then season with the sugar and some salt and pepper.

3 Preheat the oven to 200°C/180°C Fan/Gas 6. Cut the red peppers in half and remove the seeds and white pith. Divide the mince mixture between the pepper halves, place them on a baking tray and roast in the preheated oven for 25–30 minutes. Garnish with some fresh coriander before serving.

This is a great recipe that you can cook from scratch or use as a base for finishing up leftovers from a previous meal. Waste not, want not, so if you have any carrots, sprouts or other veg, throw them in. If you'd like to put some 'eggstra' effort into the presentation, then press the hash into a chef's ring to make a nice shape, but don't forget to remove the ring before serving with the eggs. People often ask me how to cook poached eggs properly. They really aren't difficult so just follow my method and you'll have cracked it! SERVES 4

MINCED BEEF HASH WITH PERFECT POACHED EGGS

700g Maris Piper
   potatoes, quartered
olive oil
300g beef mince
1 onion, thinly sliced
150g Savoy cabbage,
   shredded
2 tbsp white wine vinegar
4 free-range eggs
small bunch of fresh
   chives, chopped
sea salt
black pepper

1 Put the potatoes in a saucepan of salted water, bring to the boil and cook for 8–10 minutes. Drain the potatoes and then leave them to steam for a few minutes.

2 Heat a non-stick frying pan, add a dash of oil and fry the mince for 8–10 minutes or until browned. Add the onion to the pan and cook for another couple of minutes, then add the cabbage and potatoes. Cook over a medium to high heat until the mixture has browned, then break it up and let it brown again. The brown crust adds both flavour and texture. Season well.

3 Bring a saucepan of water to a rolling boil and add the white wine vinegar. One at a time, crack the eggs into a small bowl and tip gently into the water. Turn off the heat and leave the eggs to cook for 6–7 minutes for runny yolks. Carefully remove the eggs from the pan and place them on kitchen paper to drain. Serve the eggs on a bed of hash and sprinkle with chopped chives.

If you're not a fan of washing up, I have just the dish for you – it's all cooked in one pot! This recipe has its roots in Spain and contains red wine, smoky paprika and rich chorizo – some of my favourite ingredients. If you sometimes find couscous bland, do give this a try. The couscous takes on the other flavours in the dish, ensuring a delicious mouthful, bite after bite. SERVES 4

ONE-POT MEATBALLS WITH COUSCOUS

400g beef mince
1 tbsp breadcrumbs
1 egg yolk
2 tbsp chopped flat-leaf
    parsley
2 onions, finely chopped
olive oil
2 garlic cloves, crushed
1/2 green chilli, deseeded
    and finely diced
1/2 tsp smoked paprika
100ml red wine
1 x 400g can of
    chopped tomatoes
400ml beef stock
1 tsp sugar
200g couscous
juice of 1/2 lemon
3 tbsp chopped flat-leaf
    parsley, for garnish
sea salt
black pepper

1 Mix the mince, breadcrumbs, egg yolk, parsley and a quarter of the chopped onions in a bowl, then season with salt and pepper. Roll the mixture into about 16 golf ball-sized meatballs. Heat a non-stick pan (you need one with a lid), add a dash of oil and fry the meatballs over a medium heat until coloured all over. Remove them from the pan and set aside.

2 Add the rest of the onion, garlic, chilli and paprika to the pan and cook for a couple of minutes. Pour in the red wine and continue to cook until the liquid is reduced by half, then add the tomatoes and stock. Return the meatballs to the pan and bring everything up to the boil. Reduce the heat, cover the pan with a lid and leave to simmer for 20 minutes. Add the sugar and season with salt and pepper.

3 Add the couscous to the pan and stir it in, adding a little water if necessary. Cover the pan again and continue to cook for 5 minutes. Add the lemon juice and garnish with flat-leaf parsley before serving.

A pasta bake is such a simple idea, and almost any combination of flavours can work. I did say 'almost'. When I was at university, I had a landlady who made a tuna pasta bake with chicken soup and a topping of ready salted crisps. The less said about that the better! This recipe is a different proposition and tastes really rich and creamy, with lovely crispy chewy bits on the top. SERVES 4

BEEF AND MUSHROOM PASTA BAKE

olive oil
400g beef mince
1 onion, diced
3 garlic cloves, crushed
3 sprigs of fresh thyme (leaves picked from the stems)
3 large Portobello mushrooms, wiped and sliced
150g chestnut mushrooms, wiped and sliced
200ml white wine
300g dried farfalle pasta
60g Parmesan cheese, grated
20g breadcrumbs
3 tbsp chopped flat-leaf parsley, for serving
sea salt

White sauce
50g unsalted butter
50g plain flour
400ml milk
1 tsp English mustard
sea salt
black pepper

1 Heat a non-stick frying pan, add a dash of oil and fry the mince for 5–6 minutes until browned. Add the onion, garlic and thyme and cook for a further 3–4 minutes.

2 In another pan, fry the mushrooms with a dash of oil over a very high heat until golden. Add the white wine and cook until the liquid is reduced by half, then add the mushrooms to the beef.

3 Cook the pasta in a large pan of salted boiling water according to the packet instructions. Drain and set aside. Preheat the oven to 200°C/180°C Fan/Gas 6.

4 To make the white sauce, melt the butter over a medium heat, then whisk in the flour and cook for 2–3 minutes. Gradually pour in the milk and continue whisking until the sauce is thickened and smooth. Season with salt and pepper, then stir the mustard into the sauce.

5 Pour the sauce into the beef mixture, then mix in half of the Parmesan cheese. Pour everything into a baking dish measuring about 33 x 23cm and top with the remaining Parmesan cheese and the breadcrumbs. Bake in the preheated oven for 20 minutes or until golden, then garnish with some flat-leaf parsley before serving.

Create the fresh flavours of the Orient in your kitchen with this one-pot wonder. Don't worry if you don't have any star anise or cinnamon in your store cupboard. They are part of the Chinese five-spice blend, together with cloves, fennel seeds and Szechwan peppercorns, so the dish will still taste fine without them. I like to serve this with noodles and pak choi. **SERVES 4**

ONE-POT CHINESE BRAISED BEEF

olive oil
500g beef mince
1 onion, sliced
1 thumb-sized piece of fresh
    root ginger, peeled and
    grated
3 garlic cloves, sliced
1 red chilli, finely diced
1 star anise
½ tsp Chinese five-spice
    powder
1 cinnamon stick
1 tbsp plain flour
30ml soy sauce
80ml dry sherry
400ml beef stock
3 spring onions, sliced
1 red or green chilli, sliced

1 You need a large ovenproof pan with a lid. Heat the pan on the hob, add a dash of oil and brown the mince. I try not to break the mince up too much as I like some texture in this dish. Preheat the oven to 200°C/180°C Fan/Gas 6.

2 Add the onion, ginger, garlic, chilli, star anise and spices to the pan and cook for 5 minutes until the onion has softened. Stir in the flour and continue cooking for a couple of minutes, then pour in the soy sauce and sherry and stir until the liquid has reduced slightly. Add the beef stock, bring to the boil, then cover the pan with a lid, put it in the preheated oven and bake for about 40 minutes.

3 Garnish with some spring onions and sliced chilli before serving.

My nan, known to us all as Jack, makes a great cottage pie. It's a dish I grew up on and still enjoy to this day, but I'm definitely a bit of a chilli freak so I've injected a kick into her original. I love it! **SERVES 4**

SPICED COTTAGE PIE

Topping
500g Maris Piper
   potatoes, quartered
20g unsalted butter
60ml milk, warmed
handful of grated
   Cheddar cheese
sea salt
black pepper

Filling
olive oil
1 onion, finely chopped
1 large carrot, diced
150g mushrooms,
   wiped and sliced
3 garlic cloves, crushed
1 chilli, deseeded
   and finely diced
2 tsp ground cumin
1 tsp ground coriander
1 bay leaf
500g beef mince
600ml beef stock
2 tbsp tomato purée

1 Put the potatoes into a saucepan of salted water, bring to the boil and cook until soft, then drain. Mash with the butter and warmed milk, then season with salt and pepper.

2 For the filling, heat a non-stick frying pan, add a dash of oil and fry the onion, carrot, mushrooms, garlic and chilli for about 8 minutes until softened. Add the cumin, coriander and bay leaf, then cook for a couple more minutes.

3 Meanwhile, brown the mince with a dash of oil in a separate pan, then add it to the vegetables. Add the stock and tomato purée and simmer for 10 minutes, then season with salt and pepper. Preheat the oven to 200°C/180°C Fan/Gas 6.

4 Transfer the meat mixture to an ovenproof baking dish measuring about 33 x 23cm. Top with the potato mash, then rough up the surface with a fork and sprinkle over the grated cheese. Cook in the preheated oven for 30 minutes or until beautifully brown on top. If you prefer, you can make individual pies in small dishes. Bake at the same temperature for 20–25 minutes or until brown on top.

If you've never heard of Sloppy Joes, you've never watched *The Simpsons*. The Sloppy Joe is Homer's favourite food and I know the reason why. It's pure indulgence: mounds of beef chilli piled high into a floured roll with some red cabbage slaw on the side. Get the bibs ready – it's gonna get messy! SERVES 4

SLOPPY JOES

olive oil
500g beef mince
1 large onion, finely chopped
3 garlic cloves, crushed
1 green pepper, finely diced
200ml tomato ketchup
400ml beef stock
3 tbsp barbecue sauce
2 tbsp Worcester sauce
1 tsp English mustard
1 tsp chilli powder
1 tbsp red wine vinegar
4 rolls of your choice
mature Cheddar cheese,
   grated (optional)
soured cream (optional)
sea salt
black pepper

Red cabbage slaw
1/2 red cabbage, shredded
1 red onion, very finely sliced
1 small carrot, grated
2 tbsp chopped flat-leaf
   parsley
4 tbsp mayonnaise

1 Heat a non-stick frying pan until very hot, add a dash of oil and fry the beef for 7–8 minutes or until nicely browned. Add the onion, garlic and green pepper and cook for another 5 minutes. Then add the ketchup, stock, barbecue and Worcester sauces, mustard, chilli powder and vinegar. Stir everything together and simmer over a low to medium heat for 15–20 minutes. The mixture should be loose , so add a little more stock if needed. Season with salt and pepper.

2 To make the slaw, put the cabbage, onion, carrot and parsley in a bowl and mix well. Stir in the mayonnaise and season with salt and black pepper, then chill for 20 minutes in the fridge before serving.

3 To serve, cut the rolls in half and pile the beef mixture on top. Add some grated Cheddar cheese and a dollop of soured cream if you like, then serve with the slaw.

Hotpot is a classic dish from the heart of Lancashire. It's amazing in its own right, but I like to spice it up with some classic Tex-Mex flavours and I love the mix of textures you get from the mince and skirt steak. Great served with a dollop of soured cream and some pickled jalapeño peppers. You can cook this in individual dishes if you prefer. SERVES 4

CHILLI BEEF HOTPOT

olive oil
400g beef mince
300g skirt steak, cubed
200g mushrooms, wiped
    and thickly sliced
1 large onion, very finely diced
3 garlic cloves, crushed
1 tsp cumin seeds, ground
1 stick of cinnamon or
    ½ tsp ground cinnamon
1–2 tsp chilli powder
1 tsp dried oregano
500ml passata
1 x 400g can of red
    kidney beans
1 tbsp tomato purée
1 tbsp Worcester sauce
200ml beef stock
20g dark chocolate
    (70% cocoa), grated
sea salt
black pepper

Cheesy topping
2–3 large Maris Piper
    potatoes, sliced 5mm thick
70g Cheddar cheese, grated

1 Heat an ovenproof casserole dish, add a dash of oil and brown the mince and skirt steak, taking care not to overcrowd the pan. Do this in batches if necessary. Remove the browned meat and set it aside.

2 In the same pan, fry the mushrooms until golden, then add the onion and garlic and cook for 4–5 minutes. Add the cumin, cinnamon, chilli powder (more or less according to how hot you like your food) and oregano and cook for 1–2 minutes. Put the beef back in the pan and add the passata, beans, purée, Worcester sauce and stock. Bring to the boil, then cook over a medium heat for 10 minutes. Towards the end of the cooking time, season with salt and pepper, then add the grated chocolate.

3 For the topping, put the potatoes in a pan of salted water, bring to the boil and cook for 3–4 minutes, then drain. Preheat the oven to 180°C/160°C Fan/Gas 4.

4 Remove the cinnamon stick (if using) from the meat mixture. Arrange the potato slices on top of the meat in an overlapping pattern, then sprinkle the cheese on top. Put the dish in the preheated oven for 40–50 minutes or until the potatoes are cooked through and golden. If making individual pies, cook for 30 minutes or until golden brown on top.

I spent two years living in Falmouth, Cornwall when I was studying and I worked in a shop called Granny's Pasties. I fell in love with the traditional Cornish pasty long before then, though, during childhood holidays spent in Polzeath and St Ives. Fresh out of the oven and served with lashings of ketchup, pasties are the stuff holidays are made of. And if there any Cornish people reading this book – this is my version and I love it so please don't tell me off! Shop-bought pastry is fine if you are short of time. SERVES 4

DEAN'S PASTIES

150g Maris Piper potatoes,
   cut into 1cm cubes
150g swede, cut into
   1cm cubes
1 large onion, diced
300g beef mince
20g unsalted butter, cubed
20g Dolcelatte cheese,
   crumbled (optional)
1 egg, beaten
sea salt
loads of black pepper

Shortcrust pastry
450g plain flour, plus
   extra for rolling
good pinch of salt
200g unsalted butter, cubed
2 small eggs
30ml milk

1 First make the pastry. Sift the flour into a bowl and add the salt. Then add the butter and rub with your fingertips until the mixture has the consistency of breadcrumbs. Mix in the eggs and milk and knead to smooth dough, then wrap the pastry in cling film and chill in the fridge for about 30 minutes.

2 Roll out the pastry on a floured work surface to the thickness of a £1 coin. Using a small plate as a guide, cut the pastry into 4 rounds measuring about 15cm in diameter. Preheat the oven to 220°C/200°C Fan/Gas 7.

3 For the filling, put the cubes of potato and swede in a large bowl with the onion and season well with salt and loads of black pepper.

4 Place a quarter of the veg on the top half of a pastry circle, then add a quarter of the mince, a little of the butter and some Dolcelatte cheese (if using). Brush the edge of the pastry with water and crimp the edges together, then brush the pastry with beaten egg. Make the remaining pasties in the same way. Bake them in the preheated oven for 20 minutes, then lower the heat to 160°C/140°C Fan/Gas 3 and bake for another 40 minutes.

This recipe has been evolving for a few years as I've made a few tweaks here and there, and now it's almost perfect. The smoky flavour of the paprika-rich chorizo gives this chilli con carne a whole new dimension. Believe it or not, the chocolate is an authentic touch so don't worry – it adds a real richness to the dish. Serve with some rice, soured cream, grated Cheddar and perhaps a few jalapeños. *Arriba!* SERVES 4

BEST-EVER CHILLI CON CARNE

olive oil
500g beef mince
1 large onion, diced
4 garlic cloves, crushed
1 green pepper, deseeded
   and finely diced
130g chorizo, cut into
   1cm cubes
1 tsp ground cumin
1 cinnamon stick or
   1 tsp ground cinnamon
1–2 tsp chilli powder
   (or more to taste)
1 tsp dried oregano
2 x 400g cans of chopped
   tomatoes
1 x 400g can of red
   kidney beans
200ml beef stock
1 tsp sugar
20g dark chocolate
   (70% cocoa), grated
2 tbsp chopped fresh
   coriander, for serving
sea salt
black pepper

1 Heat a large non-stick saucepan, add a dash of oil and brown the mince. Do this in batches if necessary so you don't overcrowd the pan. Set the mince aside in a bowl and drain off any excess fat.

2 In the same pan, fry the onion, garlic, green pepper and chorizo for 3–4 minutes. Add the cumin, cinnamon, chilli powder and oregano and cook for another 1–2 minutes. Tip the mince back into the pan and add the tomatoes, kidney beans and stock. Cover the pan and cook over a low to medium heat for at least an hour – the longer you can give it the better.

3 Towards the end of the cooking time, season with salt and pepper. Check for chilli heat, adding more chilli powder if necessary, and add the sugar and grated chocolate. Sprinkle with chopped coriander before serving.

Pizzas were one of the first things that I remember cooking with my dad when I was a kid. Various toppings were laid out and we all made our own. I loved it! Pizzas are a great way to get kids involved in cooking and now I make them with Indie, my daughter. Just be prepared for lots of mess. If you haven't got time to make the dough, you can get some pretty good pizza bases from the supermarket or for a really quick version, use flour tortillas. MAKES 2 LARGE PIZZAS

SIZZLING BEEF PIZZA

Dough
500g strong bread flour,
    plus extra for dusting
1 x 7g sachet of dried yeast
1 tsp salt
30ml olive oil
300ml warm water

Topping
1 onion, finely chopped
2 garlic cloves, crushed
500ml passata
1 tsp dried oregano
1 tsp sugar
olive oil
250g beef mince
1 green chilli, sliced
20 slices of spicy pepperoni
150g ball of mozzarella
    cheese, torn
150g Cheddar cheese, grated
handful of rocket leaves,
    for serving (optional)
sea salt
black pepper

1 In a large bowl, mix the flour, yeast and salt, then add the oil. Gradually add the water and mix until a soft dough forms, then turn the dough out on to a floured surface and knead for 5 minutes. Put the dough in a clean bowl, cover with a damp tea towel and leave it in a warm place to rise for about an hour.

2 Meanwhile, fry the onion and garlic in a saucepan for 3–4 minutes. Add the passata and oregano, then cook for 2–3 minutes over a high heat until the mixture has reduced and thickened. Add the sugar and season.

3 Heat a dash of oil in a non-stick frying pan and fry the beef mince over a very high heat for 6–7 minutes or until browned.

4 Once the dough has risen, turn it out on to the worktop and knock out the air. Divide the mixture into 2 and roll each piece out on a floured surface to make circles 15–20cm wide. Preheat the oven to 240°C/220°C Fan/Gas 9 – it's important that the oven is really hot for cooking pizzas.

5 Top the pizza bases with some tomato sauce and beef, then add slices of chilli and pepperoni and dot some cheese on top. Cook the pizzas in the preheated oven for 10–12 minutes, then top with some rocket, if using, before serving.

When I was a student I have to confess that I became fond of a particular pie that was cooked in the tin it was sold in – I'm sure you know which kind I mean. I'm still partial to one of these every now and then, but when I have a bit more time on my hands I make my own version, which smashes the shop-bought one out of the water. I like to serve my pie in much the same way – brought to the table in a round enamel tin. **SERVES 4**

BEEF AND MUSHROOM ALE PIE

200g Portobello mushrooms, wiped and thickly sliced
olive oil
1 small carrot, diced
1 onion, diced
1 celery stick, diced
2 garlic cloves, crushed
400g beef mince
1 bay leaf
3 sprigs of fresh thyme
1 tbsp plain flour
300ml ale
200ml beef stock
1 tsp English mustard
1 tbsp tomato purée
1 tbsp Worcester sauce
about 300g puff pastry
1 egg, beaten
sea salt
black pepper

1 Place a non-stick frying pan over a high heat – you need one with a lid. Fry the mushrooms in a splash of oil for 6–7 minutes until they are golden. Add the carrot, onion, celery and garlic and continue to cook for 7–8 minutes, then remove the veg from the pan and set to one side. Add the mince to the pan and cook over a high heat for about 5 minutes. Lower the heat slightly, then put the veg back in the pan and add the herbs.

2 Sprinkle in the flour and cook for a minute or so, then pour in the ale. Stir with a wooden spoon to scrape up all the sticky bits from the bottom of the pan, then add just enough beef stock to cover the mixture. Stir in the mustard, tomato purée and Worcester sauce, then cover the pan with a lid and cook over a low heat for 10–15 minutes or so. Season the mixture with salt and pepper before transferring it to a pie tin about 23cm in diameter.

3 Preheat the oven to 200°C/180°C Fan/Gas 6. Roll out the pastry until it is the thickness of a £1 coin, then cut it into a circle slightly larger than your pie tin. Wet the edges of the tin with a little water, then lay the pastry over the filling. Using your fingers, crimp the pastry on to the edges of the pie tin, then trim away any excess with a knife. Brush with beaten egg, then bake in the preheated oven for 30–35 minutes. Serve hot.

These South American beauties look similar to our own Cornish pasties, but they're very different in flavour. Using punchy ingredients such as chorizo and fiery chillies guarantees a taste explosion in every bite. No two empanada recipes are the same so feel free to experiment – perhaps add some grated cheese for an added zing. I serve mine with a cooling lime and coriander dip. MAKES ABOUT 16

BEEF EMPANADAS

olive oil
400g beef mince
100g chorizo, cubed
1 small onion, finely chopped
2 garlic cloves, crushed
1 red pepper, diced
1 green chilli, deseeded
    and diced
150ml beef stock
1 x 400g can of chopped
    tomatoes
2 tbsp chopped fresh
    coriander
1 tsp ground cumin
flour, for dusting
2 x 500g packs of
    shortcrust pastry
1 egg, beaten
sea salt
black pepper

Lime and coriander dip
4 tbsp mayonnaise
juice of 1 lime
2 tbsp chopped fresh
    coriander

1 Heat a non-stick frying pan, add a dash of oil and fry the mince and chorizo for 4–5 minutes. Add the onion, garlic, pepper and chilli and continue to cook for a further 5 minutes. Pour in the stock and the tomatoes, then cook over a low heat for 5 minutes. Season, remove the pan from the heat and set the mixture aside to cool. Stir in the chopped coriander and cumin.

2 On a floured surface, roll out the pastry until it is about 5mm thick. Cut out about 16 circles of 15cm in diameter, using a small plate for a guide.

3 Place a couple of spoonfuls of the cooled filling on the top half of a pastry circle, making sure you leave a 2cm gap around the edge. Brush the exposed edge of the pastry with beaten egg, then fold over the other half and crimp the edges together with your fingers or a fork. Make the rest of the empanadas in the same way.

4 Preheat the oven to 200°C/180°C Fan/Gas 6 and grease a baking tray. Place the empanadas on the baking tray and brush them with egg. Cook in the preheated oven for 35–40 minutes and serve hot with the dip.

5 To make the dip, mix the mayonnaise, lime juice and coriander in a small bowl, then season with salt and pepper.

Have you ever seen those frozen roast dinners served up in large Yorkshire puddings in the freezer aisle in your supermarket? They gave me the idea for a twist on the classic Scottish mince and tatties which I think you'll enjoy. I have three tips for perfect Yorkshire puddings: always rest your batter for an hour; always preheat your fat; do not open the oven while they are cooking – no peeking! Serve with some buttery mash (see p. 195) and Savoy cabbage, all piled on top of the Yorkshires. **SERVES 2**

BEEF 'N' TATTIES FILLED YORKIES

olive oil
400g beef mince
1 onion, finely chopped
2 carrots, diced
2 garlic cloves, crushed
200ml red wine
300ml beef stock
1 tbsp Worcester sauce
sea salt
black pepper

Yorkshire puddings
3 eggs
120g plain flour
200ml milk
2 tbsp fresh thyme (leaves picked from the stems)
1 tbsp horseradish sauce
good pinch of sea salt
vegetable oil

1 First prepare the mince. Heat a non-stick frying pan, add a dash of oil, then add the mince and brown for 7–8 minutes. Add the onion, carrots and garlic to the pan and cook for another 7–8 minutes until softened.

2 Pour in the wine and continue to cook until the liquid is reduced by half, then add the stock and Worcester sauce. Bring the mixture back to a simmer and cook gently for 20–30 minutes. Season with salt and pepper.

3 Now make the Yorkshires. Beat the eggs in a bowl, then whisk in the flour. Add the milk, thyme and horseradish and add a good pinch of salt. Mix well, then place the batter in the fridge to rest for an hour.

4 Preheat the oven to 230°C/210°C Fan/Gas 8. Pour oil into 4 Yorkshire pudding tins measuring about 10cm across – you need enough to cover the base of the pans generously – and put them in the oven until the oil is really hot. Carefully pour the batter into the tins and cook in the oven for 25 minutes.

5 Serve 2 Yorkshire puddings per person with the mince piled up on top – and some horseradish sauce on the side, of course.

CHAPTER 2

LAMB MINCE

If I'm on a mission to eat some fantastic meatballs or a rich and spicy curry, I reach for a pack of lamb mince. Recipes such as my Moroccan-inspired meatball tagine (see p. 73) and my twist on the classic shepherd's pie with a bubble and squeak topping (see p. 76) have all become firm favourites in my house.

Like most mince, lamb mince freezes incredibly well so I always have some on hand to knock up a quick store cupboard dinner without having to go to the shops. My lamb hotpot (see p. 68) is starting to become the stuff of legends – just don't tell *Corrie*'s Betty!

This light, tomato-based sauce hides a warming chilli kick that's perfectly balanced by the sweetness of the apricots. When buying courgettes, always choose firm, heavy-feeling ones for best results. I like to serve this dish with a scattering of toasted flaked almonds on top and some fruity couscous (see p. 198). Enjoy! SERVES 4

BRAISED LAMB KOFTAS IN PIQUANT TOMATO SAUCE

2 small courgettes
olive oil
500g lamb mince
1 small onion, finely chopped
2 tbsp chopped fresh
    coriander
1 tsp cumin
½ green chilli, deseeded
    and diced
flaked almonds, for serving
3 tbsp chopped flat-leaf
    parsley, for serving
sea salt
black pepper

Sauce
olive oil
1 onion, finely chopped
3 garlic cloves, crushed
1 tsp ground cumin
1 tsp chilli powder
    (or more to taste)
500g passata
250ml lamb stock
50g dried apricots,
    finely chopped

1 Using a vegetable peeler, slice the courgettes lengthways into thin ribbons. Brush them with a little oil, then cook them on a very hot griddle pan for 2–3 minutes on each side. You may have to do this in batches.

2 Mix the lamb with the chopped onion, coriander, cumin and chilli in a large bowl and season well with salt and pepper. Form the mixture into small sausage shapes – you should have about 12. Heat a dash of oil in a non-stick frying pan and cook the koftas for 4–5 minutes until a crust forms on them – they don't need to be cooked through at this stage. Remove the koftas from the pan and leave them to cool slightly, then roll each one in a strip of courgette.

3 To make the sauce, heat a little oil in a saucepan and fry the onion and garlic over a medium heat for 8–10 minutes until golden. Add the cumin and chilli powder, then pour in the passata and stock, add the apricots and bring to simmer. Place the koftas gently into the sauce, cover the pan with a lid and cook over a low heat for 40–45 minutes.

4 Put the flaked almonds in a dry pan and toast them for a couple of minutes, watching that they don't burn. Garnish the koftas and sauce with the almonds and chopped parsley before serving.

If you crave a taste of the Mediterranean, give this simple pie a try and enjoy layers of oregano and rosemary, rich mince and aubergines, all topped with a crispy filo pastry lid. It's so easy to make and if you sit out in the sun eating this pie with a glass of white wine at your side, you'll think you've been transported to Greece. Lovely served with a courgette ribbon salad (see p. 200) and some crusty bread. SERVES 4

GREEK LAMB FILO PIE

olive oil
1 onion, finely chopped
1 carrot, diced
2 celery sticks, diced
3 garlic cloves, crushed
1 tbsp chopped fresh
   rosemary
1 tsp dried oregano
100ml white wine
500g lamb mince
150ml lamb stock
1 x 400g can of chopped
   tomatoes
1 aubergine, cut into
   5mm slices
5–6 sheets of filo pastry
30g unsalted butter, melted
sea salt
black pepper

1 Heat a non-stick frying pan, add a dash of oil and fry the onion, carrot and celery for 5–6 minutes until softened. Add the garlic, rosemary and oregano and cook for a couple more minutes, then pour in the wine and continue to cook until the liquid is reduced by half. Tip the mixture into a bowl and set aside.

2 Add a dash more oil to the pan and fry the mince until browned. Pour in the stock and stir, scraping up any sticky bits from the bottom of the pan. Add the cooked vegetables, then the tomatoes and simmer gently for 15 minutes. Season with salt and pepper.

3 Heat a griddle pan, brush the aubergine slices with oil and cook them for 1–2 minutes on each side. You will probably need to do this in batches, setting each batch aside while you cook the next. Preheat the oven to 190°C/170°C Fan/Gas 5.

4 Layer the mince mixture and aubergine slices in an ovenproof dish measuring about 33 x 23cm. Top with a sheet of filo, brush it with butter, then add a few more sheets, brushing them with butter each time and scrunching up the edges as you go. Brush the top with butter, then cook in the preheated oven for 30–35 minutes until deliciously golden and crisp on top.

This is a great one-pot dish, with fragrant spices and flavours that the whole family will enjoy. Any type of rice can be used but I find that brown basmati works best as it doesn't go all 'cakey' like other rice can during prolonged cooking times. You can serve this with a curry sauce, but I like it with just a nice wedge of lemon for squeezing. **SERVES 4**

LAMB AND MUSHROOM PILAF

olive oil
400g lamb mince
100g mushrooms, wiped
    and sliced
1 onion, sliced
1 tbsp grated fresh
    root ginger
2 garlic cloves, crushed
1 cinnamon stick
1 tbsp garam masala
1/2 tsp turmeric
250g brown basmati rice
500ml lamb stock
2 large handfuls of baby
    spinach, washed
3 tbsp chopped fresh
    coriander
wedges of lemon,
    for serving
sea salt
black pepper

1 Heat a non-stick saucepan – you need one with a lid – and add a dash of oil. Fry the lamb over a high heat for 6–7 minutes, then remove it from the pan and set aside.

2 Add a touch more oil and fry the mushrooms for 6–7 minutes until golden. Add the onion, ginger, garlic and cinnamon and continue to cook for 5 minutes. Then put the browned mince back in the pan with the spices and rice. Pour in the stock and bring to the boil, then cover the pan and cook over a low heat for 30–35 minutes or until the rice is done.

3 Lastly add the spinach and stir it through the rice and meat until wilted. Taste, then add salt and pepper if necessary – some stock is very salty. Sprinkle with fresh coriander and serve with some wedges of lemon for squeezing.

Quick and simple, this recipe is ideal for a speedy lunch or for an evening meal, served with some tabbouleh or couscous (see p. 198). The spicy harissa is perfectly balanced by the sweetness of the pomegranate seeds, which burst in your mouth like little pearls of flavour. To remove the jewel-like seeds, cut the pomegranate in half round its middle, hold it in a bowl of water and break out the seeds. This way you don't get covered in juice. This is great served with some cucumber dressing (see p. 67). SERVES 4

NORTH AFRICAN LAMB WITH POMEGRANATE

olive oil
500g lamb mince
2 garlic cloves, crushed
1/2 tsp cumin
1/2 tsp cinnamon
1 tbsp harissa paste
1 tsp honey
small squeeze of lemon juice
4 flatbreads
4 tbsp hummus
1/2 cucumber, deseeded
   and diced
1/2 red onion, sliced
2 ripe tomatoes,
   deseeded and diced
seeds from 1 pomegranate
sea salt
black pepper

1 Heat a non-stick frying pan, add a dash of oil and cook the mince for 8–10 minutes. Add the garlic, cumin, cinnamon and harissa and cook for a couple more minutes, then stir in the honey and lemon juice. Season with salt and pepper.

2 Warm the flatbreads, spread them with hummus and serve the lamb on top. Add some cucumber, onion and tomato and sprinkle with pomegranate seeds.

My simple brunch recipe is a favourite way of using up any mince left over from a previous meal. These potato cakes are light and fluffy with a crisp outer coating. Serve up with fried eggs and a steaming mug of tea to banish those morning blues. SERVES 4

POTATO CAKES

800g Maris Piper potatoes, quartered
unsalted butter
200g cooked lamb mince
1 tbsp chopped flat-leaf parsley
4 spring onions, finely sliced
3 tbsp plain flour
olive oil
4 free-range eggs
sea salt
black pepper

1 Put the potatoes in a pan of salted water, bring to the boil and cook for 8–10 minutes or until tender. Drain, put the potatoes back in the pan and leave them to stand for 5 minutes to dry slightly. Season with salt and pepper, add a knob of butter, then mash the potatoes roughly.

2 Add the lamb mince, parsley and spring onions to the pan and gently fold everything together. Shape the mixture into potato cakes, then dust them with flour.

3 Melt a knob of butter in a frying pan and cook the potato cakes for 2–3 minutes on each side or until nice and golden. Remove them from the pan and keep warm.

4 Add a little oil to the frying pan and fry the eggs until the whites are set but the yolks are still runny. Serve the eggs on top of the potato cakes.

Bobotie is to South Africa what lasagne is to Italy and moussaka to Greece. It is *the* signature dish to come out of that part of the world. This dish is lightly spiced and perfectly balanced by the sweetness of the fruit. You can find buttermilk – traditionally the liquid left behind after the butter-making process – in the dairy section of your supermarket. **SERVES 4**

BOBOTIE

2 slices of white bread,
   crusts removed
250ml buttermilk
1 egg
30g dried apricots,
   finely chopped
1 apple, grated
juice of 1/2 lemon
1/4 tsp ground cloves
olive oil
300g neck of lamb, diced
300g lamb mince
2 onions, finely chopped
2 garlic cloves, crushed
1/2 tsp turmeric
1 tbsp garam masala
unsalted butter, for greasing
8 bay leaves
sea salt
black pepper

Topping
250ml buttermilk
2 eggs, beaten

1 First tear the bread into pieces and leave to soak in the buttermilk for 5 minutes. Then beat in the egg and add the chopped apricots, grated apple, lemon juice and ground cloves. Season with salt and pepper.

2 Heat a non-stick frying pan, add a dash of oil and brown the diced lamb for 7–8 minutes. Remove and set aside, then brown the mince until golden and set aside.

3 In the same pan you used for browning the lamb, heat a little more oil and gently brown the onions for 4–5 minutes. Add the garlic, turmeric and garam masala and cook for another 1–2 minutes, then add the diced lamb, mince and the bread mixture to the pan.

4 Preheat the oven to 180°C/160°C Fan/Gas 4. Take a large ovenproof dish, about 33 x 23cm in size, and grease it with butter. Spoon in the mince mixture, poke the bay leaves into the top and bake in the oven for 30–35 minutes.

5 To make the topping, mix the buttermilk with the beaten eggs and season. Remove the bobotie from the oven, pour the topping over the meat mixture, then put the dish back in the oven and bake for a further 15 minutes or until set.

These Moroccan-influenced pittas are so tasty! The flavour comes from a blend of spices called ras el hanout, which means 'top of the shop'. It's a mix of the best spices of the day, which can include cinnamon, cloves, paprika, ginger and even rosebuds. Think of it as the Moroccan equivalent to garam masala, an Indian spice mix. Serve these succulent meatballs with my piquant cucumber dressing. **SERVES 4**

MEATBALL PITTAS WITH ZINGY CUCUMBER DRESSING

500g lamb mince
3 garlic cloves, crushed
1 tbsp finely chopped fresh
    root ginger
1/2 tsp smoked paprika
1 tbsp ras el hanout
zest of 1/2 lemon
small squeeze of lemon juice
1 large shallot or 1/2 onion,
    finely diced
olive oil
4 pitta breads, for serving
salad leaves, for serving

Cucumber dressing
1/2 cucumber, peeled,
    deseeded and diced
175g natural yoghurt
1 tsp ras el hanout
1 tbsp chopped fresh
    coriander
1 tbsp chopped fresh mint
sea salt
black pepper

1 Put the mince in a bowl with the garlic, ginger, paprika, ras el hanout, lemon zest and juice. Cover and leave to marinate for at least an hour if possible.

2 Stir the shallot into the mixture, then shape into golf ball-sized meatballs. Heat a non-stick frying pan, add a dash of oil and fry the meatballs for 7–8 minutes or until they are golden all over and cooked through.

3 For the dressing, mix the diced cucumber, yoghurt, ras el hanout and herbs in a bowl. Season with sea salt, then leave to stand for about 10 minutes before serving.

4 To serve, warm and split the pitta breads, then pack them with meatballs, salad leaves and dollops of cucumber dressing.

As I'm sure you know, lamb can be expensive. Traditionally, this dish is made with pricier cuts such as neck of lamb, but by using mince instead you can knock up an inexpensive version that still has all the flavours you love in a hotpot. SERVES 4

LAMB HOTPOT

vegetable oil
500g lamb mince
2 onions, sliced
2 sprigs of fresh thyme
   (leaves picked from
   the stems)
1 bay leaf
2 large carrots, diced
1 tbsp plain flour
500ml lamb stock
1 tbsp Worcester sauce
3 large Maris Piper potatoes,
   cut into 5mm slices
30g unsalted butter, melted
sea salt
black pepper

1 You'll need an ovenproof casserole dish with a lid for cooking this recipe. Heat the casserole dish on the hob, add a splash of vegetable oil, then brown the mince. You may have to do this in batches so you don't overcrowd the pan. Remove the mince and set it aside.

2 Add the sliced onions, thyme, bay leaf and carrots to the casserole dish and cook until browned and softened. This will take about 5 minutes. Sprinkle in the flour and cook for a minute or so, then add the stock and Worcester sauce. Bring everything to the boil and season with salt and black pepper.

3 Preheat the oven to 180°C/160°C Fan/Gas 4. Put the sliced potatoes in a pan of salted water, bring to the boil and cook for 3–4 minutes, then drain. When the potato slices are cool enough to handle, place them over the surface of the meat in neat overlapping rows. Season with salt and black pepper.

4 Place the lid on the casserole and put it in the preheated oven for 1½ hours. Take the dish out, remove the lid and brush the potatoes with the melted butter. Put the dish back in the oven for 20–25 minutes or until the potatoes are crisp.

Spanakopita is a famous Greek dish – a rich spinach-and-cheese-filled wonder. It's sometimes served in small triangles, but I like to make it in one big dish so the family can help themselves. The filo is very easy to work with and you don't even have to be neat – the messier the better, I say. Great served with some minty tzatziki (see p. 203). **SERVES 6**

MEATY LAMB SPANAKOPITA

olive oil
1 small onion, finely sliced
2 garlic cloves, crushed
400g lamb mince
300g baby spinach, washed
150g feta cheese, crumbled
50g pine nuts, toasted in a
    dry pan for a minute or so
2 eggs, beaten
1 tsp dried oregano
small grating of nutmeg
squeeze of lemon juice
6 or 7 sheets of filo pastry
100g unsalted butter, melted
sea salt
black pepper

1 Heat a non-stick frying pan, add a dash of oil and fry the onion and garlic for 2–3 minutes or until softened. Remove the onion and garlic from the pan and set aside, then crank up the heat to high and cook the lamb mince until golden.

2 Put the spinach in a large saucepan and cover with a lid. Place it on the heat until the leaves have wilted down – this doesn't take long. Drain the spinach and squeeze out as much of the excess water as you can, then leave to cool. Chop the cooled spinach roughly and put it in a bowl. Add the cooked onion and garlic, browned lamb mince and the feta, pine nuts, eggs, oregano, nutmeg and lemon juice. Mix everything together well and season with salt and pepper. Preheat the oven to 190°C/170°C Fan/Gas 5.

3 Take a sheet of filo, brush it with melted butter and lay it in an ovenproof dish. Add a few more sheets of filo, brushing each one with butter and allowing them to hang over the edges of the dish. Put the mince and spinach mixture into the dish, then fold the filo pastry over the filling. Lay a couple more sheets of filo on top and brush them with butter. Bake in the oven for 30–35 minutes.

A burger can be adapted in almost any way you want. Just take your favourite flavour combinations and go for it. Home-made burgers are so superior in terms of taste and texture that once you start to make them you will never go back to the frozen variety. Lamb, mint and salty feta cheese is one of my favourite combos. Serve with a feta and beetroot salad (see p. 201) and you have an amazing dinner. SERVES 4

MINTY LAMB BURGERS

400g lamb mince
1/2 red onion, chopped
2 tbsp chopped fresh mint
50g fresh breadcrumbs
40g feta cheese, crumbled
olive oil
sea salt
black pepper

Pea salsa
200g frozen peas, defrosted
1/2 red onion, diced
1/2 red chilli, deseeded
 and diced
2 tbsp chopped mint
30ml olive oil
juice of 1/2 lime

1 Put the lamb mince in a bowl and mix in the onion, mint, breadcrumbs and crumbled feta. Season, divide the mixture into 4, then shape into burgers.

2 Heat a non-stick frying pan, add a dash of oil and cook the burgers over a medium heat for 6–7 minutes on each side. Alternatively, you can barbecue them if you prefer.

3 To make the pea salsa, tip the peas into a bowl and crush them with a spoon. Stir in the onion, chilli and mint, then the oil and lime juice.

This is my take on a Moroccan lamb tagine, a dish that has a perfect balance of fiery and fruity flavours. One tip on harissa – do taste it before cooking, as some are much hotter than others. Serve this with some herby couscous (see p. 198). SERVES 4

MOROCCAN MEATBALL TAGINE

Meatballs
400g lamb mince
½ onion, very finely chopped
2 garlic cloves, crushed
1 tbsp harissa paste
30g fresh breadcrumbs
1 tbsp chopped flat-leaf
    parsley, plus extra
    for serving
olive oil
sea salt
black pepper

Sauce
olive oil
½ onion, finely chopped
4 garlic cloves, crushed
1 tbsp finely chopped fresh
    root ginger
1 tsp paprika
1 tsp ground cinnamon
1 tsp coriander seeds, crushed
1 x 400g can of chopped
    tomatoes
140ml chicken stock
60g dried apricots, chopped
1 tbsp honey

1 Mix the mince, onion, garlic, harissa paste, breadcrumbs and flat-leaf parsley together in a bowl and season. Roll the mixture into about 16 golf ball-sized meatballs, place them on a plate and cover with cling film. Chill the meatballs in the fridge for 30 minutes.

2 Heat a non-stick frying pan, add a dash of oil and fry the meatballs until coloured – this should take 4–5 minutes.

3 To make the sauce, heat a little oil in a heavy-based saucepan and fry the onion, garlic and ginger for 7–8 minutes until softened. Add the spices and cook for a further 1–2 minutes, then add the tomatoes, stock and apricots. Tip the meatballs into the sauce, cover the pan with a lid and cook for 30 minutes. After 20 minutes, add the honey and season with salt and pepper. Sprinkle on some more parsley before serving.

Shepherd's pie is a British classic and the ultimate in comfort food, but my version has the extra treat of a cheesy bubble and squeak topping. I'm sure you are all familiar with bubble and squeak but if not, it's a dish made with leftover vegetables such as potatoes, cabbage, carrots, sprouts – anything goes. I love the texture this combo gives to a shepherd's pie and I always make mine like this now. **SERVES 4**

SHEPHERD'S PIE WITH BUBBLE AND SQUEAK TOPPING

olive oil
1 large carrot, diced
1 celery stick, diced
2 garlic cloves, crushed
1 tbsp finely chopped
   fresh rosemary
500g lamb mince
200ml white wine
300ml lamb stock
1 tbsp tomato purée
1 tsp cornflour mixed
   with 1 tsp cold water
sea salt
black pepper

Topping
500g Maris Piper
   potatoes, quartered
½ Savoy cabbage, shredded
20g unsalted butter
60ml milk, warmed
1 tbsp wholegrain mustard
100g Cheddar cheese,
   grated

1 First make the topping. Put the potatoes in a pan of salted water, bring to the boil and cook until tender. Drain them, then mash. Add the cabbage to a pan of salted boiling water and cook for 1–2 minutes, then drain and add it to the mash. Mix in the butter, warmed milk and mustard and season with salt and pepper.

2 Heat a non-stick frying pan, add a dash of oil and fry the diced veg, garlic and rosemary for about 10 minutes. Remove and set aside, then brown the mince – in batches if necessary. Add the vegetables to the pan with the mince, then pour in the white wine. Cook until the wine has reduced by half, then add the stock and tomato purée and simmer for 10 minutes. Add the cornflour mixture and stir until thickened. Season with salt and pepper. Preheat the oven to 200°C/180°C Fan/Gas 6.

3 Transfer the meat mixture to an ovenproof baking dish measuring about 33 x 23cm and top with the potato and cabbage mash. Roughen up the surface with a fork, then sprinkle over the grated cheese. Place in the preheated oven for 30 minutes or until lovely and brown on top.

I was shown how to make this amazing Greek dish while filming *Take on the Takeaway* a few years ago. The Lemon Tree restaurant and takeaway in London made it for me and it blew me away. I've simplified my version but it's still just as tasty. Serve with my pea and feta salad below and some tzatziki (see p. 203). SERVES 2

SHEFTALIA WITH PEA AND FETA SALAD

500g lamb mince
1 onion, grated
2 garlic cloves, crushed
3 tbsp chopped flat-leaf
    parsley
1 tsp dried oregano
juice of $\frac{1}{2}$ lemon
olive oil
sea salt
black pepper

Pea and feta salad
250g frozen peas, defrosted
4 spring onions, finely sliced
100g baby spinach, washed
2 tbsp chopped fresh mint
juice of $\frac{1}{2}$ lemon
30ml olive oil
100g feta cheese

1 Put the lamb mince in a bowl and add the grated onion. Mix in the garlic, parsley, oregano and lemon juice, then season with salt and pepper. Knead thoroughly until the ingredients are well mixed, then mould into 8 sausage shapes. Cover them with cling film and leave to chill in the fridge for 30 minutes.

2 Heat a non-stick pan, add a dash of oil and fry the sheftalia for 13–15 minutes. Turn them until coloured on all sides and cooked through.

3 To make the salad, mix the peas with the spring onions, spinach and mint. Dress with the lemon juice and olive oil, then season with salt and pepper and crumble the feta cheese on top. Serve with the salad.

Moroccan flavourings remind me of hot summer evenings spent cooking with the family. Even just the smell of spices such as cumin and cinnamon cooking makes me very happy... My lamb burgers are served with a harissa and carrot slaw. Harissa is a North African spice paste which can be very fiery, so add as much or little as you can handle. SERVES 4

MOROCCAN LAMB BURGERS

olive oil
½ onion, diced
2 garlic cloves, crushed
1 tbsp finely chopped
   fresh root ginger
500g lamb mince
1 tbsp ras el hanout
1 tsp ground cinnamon
zest of ½ lemon
4 burger buns
salad leaves, for serving
sea salt
black pepper

Harissa and carrot slaw
2 carrots
1 red onion, sliced
3 tbsp mayonnaise
1 tsp harissa paste
small drizzle of honey
small squeeze of lemon juice
1 tbsp chopped fresh mint

1 Heat a non-stick frying pan, add a dash of oil and fry the onion, garlic and chopped ginger for 4–5 minutes over a medium heat without letting them colour. Leave to cool, then mix with the mince, spices and lemon zest. Season with salt and pepper. Shape into 4 patties, cover with cling film and chill them in the fridge for 30 minutes before cooking.

2 To make the slaw, grate the carrots into a large bowl, then sprinkle them with salt and leave to stand for 10 minutes. Squeeze out any excess liquid from the carrot, then mix in the rest of the ingredients. Leave the slaw to stand for at least 10 minutes for the flavours to develop before serving.

3 Add a little more oil to the frying pan if you need and cook the burgers for 7–8 minutes on each side or until cooked through. Meanwhile, toast the buns and serve the burgers on the buns with the slaw and some salad leaves.

I've been working on this, my version of the Greek classic moussaka, for a while. I thought I'd cracked it until recently when I sampled some cooked by a lovely Greek lady at a food festival and it was back to the drawing board. I've definitely got it right now, but rather than cooking a traditional cheesy white sauce I've made a simple yoghurt topping. This way you can get it to the table quicker to tuck in! SERVES 4

MOUTHWATERING MOUSSAKA

1 aubergine, cut lengthways
   into 1cm slices
olive oil
2 medium potatoes,
   cut into 1cm slices
500g lamb mince
1 onion, finely diced
3 garlic cloves, crushed
150ml white wine
1 x 400g can of chopped
   tomatoes
1 tbsp tomato purée
150ml lamb stock
1 tbsp dried oregano
1 tbsp chopped fresh mint
1/2 tsp ground cinnamon
1 tsp sugar
sea salt
black pepper

Topping
200g Greek natural yoghurt
100g feta cheese, crumbled
1 egg, beaten
small grating of nutmeg

1 Brush both sides of the aubergine slices with oil and season them with salt and pepper. Grill the slices for 3–4 minutes until coloured, then turn them and grill on the other side for 3 minutes. Set the slices aside. Meanwhile, put the sliced potatoes in a pan of boiling water and cook for 3–4 minutes. Drain, then set aside.

2 Heat a non-stick frying pan, add a dash of oil and brown the lamb mince until golden – this should take 6–7 minutes. Remove the lamb from the pan and set aside, then add the onion and garlic and cook for 5–6 minutes. Pour in the white wine to deglaze the pan, scraping up all the sticky bits, then put the lamb mince back in and add the rest of the ingredients. Bring to a simmer, then cook with a lid on for 15 minutes.

3 To make the topping, mix the yoghurt, feta, egg and nutmeg in a small bowl and season. Preheat the oven to 190°C/170°C Fan/Gas 5.

4 Take an ovenproof dish measuring about 33 x 23cm. Spread a third of the mince mixture in the dish, then top with potato slices and season. Add another layer of mince, then the aubergine slices and top with the rest of the mince. Pour over the yoghurt and feta mixture and cook in the preheated oven for 50 minutes.

A Malay bredie is a spicy stew that originated in South Africa. This is another recipe passed down in my family by my nan Judith, who came over to Britain from Cape Town in the 1960s. No family party went by without all of us enjoying a massive pot of this bredie, and I think eating this meal is one of my earliest and fondest food memories. Traditionally made with cubed shoulder of lamb, mince is a great budget-friendly substitute. Serve with rice or my favourite accompaniment – some roast potatoes (see p. 196). **SERVES 4**

MALAY LAMB BREDIE

olive oil
600g lamb mince
2 medium onions,
    finely chopped
3 garlic cloves, crushed
1 tsp ground cumin
1 tsp chilli powder
    (or more to taste)
2 courgettes, sliced
1 x 400g can of tomatoes
2 tbsp tomato purée
300ml lamb stock
1 tbsp sugar
3 tbsp chopped flat-leaf
    parsley
sea salt
black pepper

1 Preheat a large saucepan, add a dash of oil and brown the lamb – this will take 7–8 minutes. Try not to break the mince up too much as it's nice to keep a bit of texture. Remove the browned mince from the pan and set aside.

2 Add the onions to the pan and fry over a medium heat for 8–10 minutes until golden. Add the garlic, cumin and chilli powder.

3 Put the lamb back in the pan and add the courgettes, canned tomatoes, tomato purée and stock. Bring to a simmer, then cover the pan and cook the stew over a low heat for 50 minutes. Ten minutes before the end of the cooking time, add the sugar and season with salt and pepper. Just before serving, stir in the flat-leaf parsley.

The infamous doner kebab has been around for a good few years and, like most takeaway foods, you find good and bad versions. Try my home-made doner with lashings of fresh salad and hot chilli sauce. I was shown how to make this chilli sauce recipe a few years back by a very kind Turkish guy and it tastes great. Do give it a try. SERVES 4

DEAN'S DONER KEBABS

500g lamb mince
50ml natural yoghurt
2 garlic cloves, crushed
1 tsp smoked paprika
1 tsp ground cumin
½ tsp ground cinnamon
½ tsp dried oregano
50g fresh breadcrumbs
juice and zest of ½ lemon
olive oil
4 flatbreads
small tub of hummus
½ cucumber, deseeded
    and diced
½ red onion, sliced
2 ripe tomatoes,
    deseeded and diced

Hot chilli sauce
4 garlic cloves, crushed
½ red onion, diced
2 red chillies, roughly chopped
1 fresh tomato, diced
1 red pepper, chopped
1 tsp dried chilli flakes
2 tbsp tomato purée
1 tbsp white wine vinegar
sea salt

1 In a large bowl, mix the lamb mince with the yoghurt, garlic, spices, oregano, breadcrumbs and lemon. Shape the mixture into golf ball-sized meatballs, then chill them for at least 20 minutes.

2 Heat a non-stick frying pan, add a dash of oil and cook the meatballs over a medium heat for 12–14 minutes or until cooked through.

3 Place all the ingredients for the sauce in a blender and blitz until you have a fine paste. Tip the paste into a saucepan and cook gently for 3–4 minutes, adding a little water to loosen if required. Season with a touch of salt.

4 Toast the flatbreads and spread them with a dollop of hummus. Add the meatballs and some cucumber, onion and tomato, then as much chilli sauce as you can handle!

If you are looking for a Thai curry that doesn't contain high-fat coconut milk, this is the recipe for you. It still packs the flavours you associate with Thai food but it's cooked in a tomato-rich sauce. I first tried this dish in a local Thai restaurant and fell in love with it so just had to come up with my own recipe. If you don't have palm sugar and fish sauce, use brown sugar and soy sauce. If you find some lime leaves, use what you need, then freeze the rest and use them straight from frozen next time. Serve this with some jasmine rice (see p. 199). **SERVES 4**

THAI LAMB AND TOMATO CURRY

2 large shallots, chopped
500g lamb mince
2 tbsp chopped fresh
    coriander, plus extra
    for garnish
1 tbsp red Thai curry paste
vegetable oil
1 tbsp chopped fresh
    root ginger
3 garlic cloves, crushed
1 red chilli, diced
4 Kaffir lime leaves
2 lemon grass stalks
1 tbsp palm sugar
1–2 tbsp nam pla (fish sauce)
1 x 400g can of
    chopped tomatoes
1 tbsp tomato purée
200ml chicken stock
juice of 1 lime

1 Mix half the chopped shallots with the lamb mince, 2 tablespoons of fresh coriander and Thai paste. Roll the mixture into small meatballs, then cover with cling film and chill them in the fridge for 20 minutes.

2 Heat a dash of oil in a large non-stick saucepan and cook the meatballs for 6–7 minutes. Add the rest of the shallots and the ginger, garlic, chilli and lime leaves, then bash the lemon grass stalks with a rolling pin and add them to the pan. Cook for another 3–4 minutes.

3 Sprinkle in the sugar and give everything a quick stir before pouring in the fish sauce, chopped tomatoes, purée and stock. Bring to the boil, then simmer gently for 30–35 minutes.

4 Remove the lemon grass and lime leaves, squeeze in the lime juice and garnish with the extra coriander before serving.

Sunday lunch with all the family is one of the great food occasions, but it doesn't seem to happen often enough these days. I want to change that, starting with this recipe for a budget-conscious lamb roast. Breast of lamb is a cheap but tasty cut of meat and stuffing it with the zesty mince filling makes it go further and adds tremendous flavour. Serve with the usual suspects of roast potatoes (see p. 196), cabbage, gravy (see p. 202) and of course loads of mint sauce. **SERVES 4**

ROSEMARY-STUFFED BREAST OF LAMB

olive oil
1 onion, very finely diced
2 garlic cloves, crushed
1 tbsp finely chopped
   rosemary
200g lamb mince
80g fresh breadcrumbs
grated zest of 1 lemon
1 breast of lamb,
   trimmed of excess fat
1 tbsp Dijon mustard
sea salt
black pepper

1 Heat a non-stick frying pan, add a dash of oil and gently fry the onion until softened. Add the garlic and rosemary and cook for another 2–3 minutes, then leave to cool slightly.

2 Put the mince, breadcrumbs and lemon zest in a bowl, stir in the onion mixture and season with salt and pepper. Lay the trimmed breast of lamb on a board and paint it with the mustard. Spread the stuffing mixture on top and roll up the meat tightly. Tie it with string at 3cm intervals so that it holds together while cooking. Preheat the oven to 190°C/170°C Fan/Gas 5.

3 Heat a roasting tin on top of the stove and quickly brown the joint all over. Transfer the tin to the preheated oven and roast the lamb for about $1\frac{1}{2}$ hours. Remove from the oven, cover the lamb with foil and leave to rest for 10 minutes before carving.

Let's be honest – we all love a takeaway every now and then. My favourite is a scorching hot morich masala from my local curry house, Blue Ginger, which specializes in Bengal food. This is my version of their curry, which combines lamb mince and chicken. It might sound strange but for me it's the best of both worlds. Serve with some pilaf rice (see p. 199) and naan bread to mop up the juices. **SERVES 4**

MORICH MASALA

2 skinless chicken breasts
olive oil
500g lamb mince
2 large onions, diced
4 garlic cloves, crushed
1 tbsp grated fresh root ginger
1 green pepper, deseeded
   and chopped into 8 pieces
1 tbsp garam masala
1 tsp ground cumin
1 tsp ground coriander
1 tsp turmeric
1 tsp ground fenugreek
3–4 green bullet chillies,
   halved
400ml lamb stock
2 tbsp tomato purée
3 spring onions, sliced
1 tbsp chopped fresh
   coriander, to garnish
sea salt
black pepper

1 Preheat the oven to 200°C/180°C Fan/Gas 6. Season the chicken breasts with salt and pepper. Heat a small ovenproof pan that you can use on the hob, add a dash of oil and seal the chicken breasts for 2–3 minutes. Turn them over, transfer the pan to the oven and cook the chicken for 10 minutes.

2 Meanwhile, heat a little oil in a non-stick pan – you need one with a lid – and fry the lamb mince over a high heat until golden. Add the onions, garlic, ginger and green pepper and cook for another 6–7 minutes. Add the spices and chillies to taste, then cook for a couple more minutes.

3 Slice the cooked chicken breasts lengthways and add them the pan with any resting juices. Stir in the stock and tomato purée, cover the pan with a tight-fitting lid and simmer for 10–15 minutes. Before serving, take out the chillies if you like and stir in the spring onions and garnish with fresh coriander.

These quick and easy snacks make a great prepare-ahead starter for a dinner party and they're also a godsend if friends drop over and need a snack. I like to serve them with a salad and a cooling yoghurt dip (see raita on p. 156). If you'd like to make a slightly healthier version, bake the samosas in a preheated oven at 180°C/160°C Fan/Gas 4 for 20–25 minutes or until golden brown. MAKES ABOUT 16

SOUTH AFRICAN SAMOSAS

vegetable oil
500g lamb mince
1 onion, very finely diced
3 garlic cloves, crushed
1 tbsp grated fresh root ginger
1 tsp ground cumin
½ tsp chilli powder
½ tsp turmeric
2 tbsp chopped fresh coriander
8 sheets of filo pastry
40g unsalted butter, melted
sea salt
black pepper

1 Heat a non-stick frying pan, add a dash of oil and brown the lamb mince. You might need to do this in batches so you don't overcrowd the pan. Remove the meat and set aside.

2 Add a little more oil if necessary and fry the onion, garlic and ginger for 5 minutes until softened. Add the spices and cook for another 1–2 minutes. Put the mince back in the pan and continue cooking for 4–5 minutes. Season with salt and pepper, then leave to cool slightly. Add the chopped coriander.

3 Cut a sheet of filo in half. Take 1 strip and place a spoonful of mince in the bottom corner. Fold the corner over to make a triangle, then continue folding corner to corner until you reach the top of the filo. Brush the edge with melted butter to seal the edges of the final fold.

4 Heat some vegetable oil in a frying pan and shallow-fry the samosas, a few at a time, over a medium heat. Fry for 4–5 minutes, turning until golden brown.

I love mint sauce and often use it instead of fresh mint in home-cooked dishes. I can't tell you why it works – it just does. Serve these puddings with some buttery mashed potatoes (see p. 195), minted peas and more mint sauce on the side. You need four individual pudding basins. SERVES 4

LAMB AND MINT PUDDINGS

olive oil
1 carrot, diced
1 onion, diced
1 celery stick, diced
80g chestnut mushrooms, wiped and sliced
1 bay leaf
400g lamb mince
1 tbsp plain flour
250ml ale
150ml lamb stock
1 tbsp mint sauce
unsalted butter, for greasing
sea salt
black pepper

Suet pastry
300g self-raising flour
150g beef suet
12–14 tbsp ice-cold water

1 Heat a non-stick frying pan, add a little oil and fry the carrot, onion, celery, mushrooms and bay leaf until the veg have softened. This should take 6–7 minutes. Remove the veg from the pan and set aside, then brown the mince.

2 Put the vegetables back in the pan with the lamb and stir in the flour. Cook for a couple of minutes, then pour in the ale to deglaze the pan, scraping up all the sticky bits. Pour in enough stock just to cover and stir in the mint sauce to taste. Cover the pan with a lid and cook over a low heat for 40–50 minutes. Season with salt and pepper, then leave to cool.

3 To make the suet pastry, sift the flour and mix it with the suet, then season with salt and pepper. Add the water, 1 tablespoon at a time, and mix until the pastry comes together. Do not overwork it. Wrap the pastry in cling film and chill it in the fridge for 30 minutes.

4 Roll out the pastry to about 5mm thick and cut out 4 circles to fit inside your pudding basins. Then cut out 4 more circles slightly larger than the tops of the basins to make the lids.

5 Grease the pudding basins with butter, then line each basin with a circle of pastry. Fill the basins two-thirds full with the lamb mixture. Wet the rim of the pastry with cold water and top with a pastry lid, then crimp the edges together and trim off any excess. Cover each basin with some foil, making a pleat in the middle to allow for the pudding's expansion, and tie the foil in place with string.

6 Put the basins in a large pan and pour in boiling water to come halfway up the basins. Cover the pan with a lid and steam the puddings for 1 hour. Keep checking and add more boiling water when necessary. Don't let the pan boil dry.

7 At the end of the cooking time, carefully remove the puddings from the pan. Remove the string and foil. Using a knife, gently loosen each pudding from the basin all the way round and turn out on to plates. Serve at once.

Although this recipe is Greek in its flavourings I first ate it in the United States. It might sound a little strange but trust me – the salty feta is perfectly offset by the sweet and juicy watermelon. It is to die for! I'm no drinks expert but serving this one up at a garden party along with a jug of well-chilled Pimm's is what summer is all about. SERVES 4

LAMB WITH FETA AND WATERMELON SALAD

Meatballs
400g lamb mince
3 garlic cloves, crushed
1 tsp dried oregano
1 tbsp chopped fresh mint
grated zest of $1/2$ lemon
50g feta cheese, crumbled
olive oil
black pepper

Salad
$1/2$ ripe watermelon
olive oil
40g pine nuts
150g feta cheese crumbled
1 red onion, sliced
2 tbsp mint leaves, shredded,
    plus extra for garnish

Dressing
100ml natural yoghurt
1 tbsp chopped mint
$1/2$ tsp ground cumin
juice of $1/2$ lemon
pinch of sugar
sea salt
black pepper

1 Mix the lamb, garlic, herbs, lemon zest and feta in a large bowl and add a good grinding of black pepper. You probably won't need salt, as the feta should be salty enough. Roll the mixture into small meatballs, cover with cling film and leave them in the fridge to chill for 15–20 minutes. Heat a non-stick frying pan, add a dash of oil and cook the meatballs for 8–10 minutes or until they are coloured and cooked through. Set them aside and keep warm.

2 Meanwhile, slice the watermelon, remove the peel and seeds and cut the flesh into 5cm squares, about 1–2cm thick. Lightly brush the melon squares with oil, then place them on a very hot preheated griddle pan for about 2 minutes. Turn them over and cook for 2 minutes on the other side. Toast the pine nuts in a dry pan until lightly coloured, keeping a close eye on them so they don't burn.

3 Mix the dressing ingredients together in a jug and season with salt and pepper. Place the meatballs in a serving bowl. Arrange the griddled watermelon, feta, onion and mint on a large platter, then garnish with the pine nuts and some more mint leaves. Add the yoghurt dressing and add a good drizzle of olive oil, then serve immediately.

CHAPTER 3

PORK MINCE

Pork mince is very versatile and works with other flavours incredibly well. In this chapter I have taken influences from many corners of the world, from Southeast Asia for my wonderfully spicy pork and butternut laksa (see p. 114) to Italy for my pesto meatball pasta (see p. 102).

I couldn't do a pork chapter without including a recipe for Scotch eggs (see p. 129) – semi-set yolk and a meaty filling encased in a crispy breadcrumb crust. What more could you want? Done right, Scotch eggs are my ultimate comfort food and well on a par with a juicy burger. Bear in mind that pork mince can have quite a high fat content so you may not always need to add oil when cooking.

For a taste of the American deep south, in particular New Orleans, here is my take on a classic Creole dish – jambalaya. Loosely translated, it means 'jumbled', which is great as you can add whatever ingredients you like, such as chicken and spicy sausage. This is a great one-pot dish to feed the whole family and you can even add some fresh chilli for the heat-seekers! SERVES 4

CREOLE JAMBALYA

300g pork mince
olive oil
200g chorizo, diced
1 onion, finely diced
3 garlic cloves, crushed
1 red pepper, finely diced
1 green pepper, finely diced
2 bay leaves
½ tsp turmeric
1 tsp smoked paprika
1 tsp cumin
200ml white wine
1 x 400g can of
    chopped tomatoes
350g brown basmati rice
1 litre chicken stock
    (more if required)
100g shelled raw prawns
3 tbsp chopped flat-leaf
    parsley
4 spring onions, sliced
soured cream (optional)
sea salt
black pepper

1 Season the pork mince and roll it into small, bite-sized meatballs. Heat a large pan, add a dash of oil and brown the meatballs all over for 7–8 minutes. Remove the meatballs from the pan and set to one side.

2 Add the diced chorizo, onion, garlic and peppers to the pan and cook for another 5 minutes. Then add the bay leaves, turmeric, paprika and cumin and stir for a minute before pouring in the white wine and tomatoes.

3 Add the rice to the pan and stir well. Heat the stock in a separate pan, add it to the rice and meatballs and bring to a simmer. Cover the pan with a lid and cook the jambalaya over the lowest heat for 30–35 minutes or until the rice is cooked. Keep an eye on the liquid level and add more stock if required.

4 When the rice is done, stir in the prawns and cook for 3–4 minutes or until they turn pink. Before serving, stir in the parsley and spring onions, then season to taste. Serve with a big dollop of soured cream if you like.

Once you've got all your ingredients ready, this dish can be cooked very quickly. Italians really understand the meaning of fast food. You can use any sort of pasta you like but I love farfalle for this recipe. The name of this pasta means 'butterflies', although this pasta shape is also known as 'bow ties', and they hold the garlicky sauce well. SERVES 4

GARLICKY PORK AND COURGETTE FARFALLE

20g unsalted butter
2 courgettes, sliced
3 garlic cloves, crushed
400g pork mince
olive oil
400g dried farfalle pasta
1 red onion, diced
100g cherry tomatoes, halved
1 red chilli, deseeded and
    finely diced
150ml white wine
2 tbsp crème fraiche
1/2 a lemon
2 handfuls of rocket leaves
lemon wedges, for serving
sea salt
black pepper

1 Put a large pan of salted water on to boil for the pasta. Melt the butter in another large pan and fry the courgettes for 6–7 minutes. Throw in the garlic and cook for another minute. Remove the courgettes and garlic from the pan and set aside.

2 Meanwhile, brown the pork mince with a dash of oil in another pan – this will take 10–12 minutes.

3 While the mince is cooking, cook the pasta in the salted water according to the packet instructions. Drain and set aside.

4 In the pan you used for cooking the courgettes, fry the onion, tomatoes and chilli for 3–4 minutes, then add the white wine and continue cooking until the liquid is reduced by half. Stir in the crème fraiche and add a good squeeze of lemon juice. Add the mince and courgettes to the pan, toss in the rocket and stir to combine. Add the drained pasta and toss it through the sauce. Check the seasoning and serve with lemon wedges on the side.

Pork mince is relatively inexpensive but the golden rule still applies – buy the best quality that you can afford. You can use any leftover meatballs and sauce with some pasta for your dinner the following evening so you get two meals for the price of one! SERVES 4

MEATBALL SUB MELT

400g pork mince
1 tsp smoked paprika
1 tbsp chopped flat-leaf
  parsley
30g fresh breadcrumbs
olive oil
4 sub rolls
Gruyère cheese
Parmesan cheese, grated
sea salt
black pepper

Sauce
olive oil
1 red onion, roughly chopped
2 garlic cloves, crushed
1 tbsp fresh thyme (leaves
  picked from the stems)
200ml red wine
500ml passata
1 tbsp barbecue sauce
2 tbsp balsamic vinegar
1 tsp sugar

1 In a large bowl, mix the pork mince, paprika, parsley and breadcrumbs thoroughly and season with salt and pepper. Shape the mixture into golf ball-sized meatballs, then cover with cling film and leave them to chill in the fridge for about 30 minutes.

2 To make the sauce, heat a dash of oil in a saucepan and gently fry the onion, garlic and thyme for 5–6 minutes. Add the red wine and continue cooking until the liquid is reduced by half, then pour in the passata, barbecue sauce and balsamic vinegar. Leave to simmer for 10 minutes. Season with the sugar and a good pinch of salt and pepper.

3 Heat a frying pan with a little oil and fry the meatballs for 6–7 minutes or until a crust has formed on the outside. Transfer the browned meatballs to the sauce, cover the pan with a lid and cook for another 20–25 minutes.

4 Slice the sub rolls in half but don't cut right the way through. Place some slices of Gruyère cheese on the bottom half of each sub roll. Add some meatballs and sauce, top with some grated Parmesan and prepare to get messy!

My brother Wes and I have always loved sweet and sour pork. This recipe is my shot at a great home-cooked version and much fresher tasting and healthier than your average takeaway. Hope Wes approves! SERVES 4

SWEET AND SOUR PORK BALLS

400g pork mince
1 tsp Chinese 5-spice
  powder
2 tbsp soy sauce
50g fresh breadcrumbs
4 tbsp chopped fresh
  coriander
olive oil
3 spring onions,
  finely sliced

Sweet and sour sauce
2 garlic cloves, crushed
1 tbsp grated fresh root
  ginger
50ml white wine vinegar
50g soft brown sugar
4 tbsp tomato ketchup
300ml chicken stock
1 tsp cornflour
2 tsp water
1 tbsp soy sauce

*Broccoli, beansprouts
  and noodles*
300g dried egg noodles
olive oil
200g purple sprouting
  broccoli
100g beansprouts
2 eggs, beaten

1 Put the pork mince in a bowl and mix it with the 5-spice, soy sauce, breadcrumbs and half the fresh coriander. Shape the mixture into meatballs, then cover with cling film and chill them in the fridge for 20 minutes if you have time. Heat a non-stick pan, add a dash of oil and fry the meatballs for 12–14 minutes or until cooked through. Remove them from the pan and set aside.

2 To make the sauce, add the garlic and ginger to the pan and cook over a medium heat for 1–2 minutes. Then add the vinegar, sugar, ketchup and stock and give everything a good stir. Mix the cornflour and water in a bowl, then add the mixture to the sauce and stir until thickened. Add the soy sauce.

3 Cook the noodles in boiling water according to the packet instructions, then drain and set aside. Heat a little oil in a non-stick wok or large pan and fry the purple sprouting broccoli for 4 minutes or until cooked through. Add the noodles and beansprouts, then push them to the side of the pan and add the beaten eggs. Cook the eggs for about 30 seconds, then fold them into the noodles.

4 Stir the meatballs into the sweet and sour sauce, then garnish with the spring onions and the rest of the fresh coriander. Serve with the broccoli, beansprouts and noodles.

I am a massive fan of the classic insalata Caprese – tomato, mozzarella and basil salad to you and me. It's amazing how a dish so simple can be so good. I've combined all these ingredients along with a zingy fresh pesto to create one of my all-time favourite pasta dishes. This quick pesto beats any shop-bought version by a long way so do give it a go. **SERVES 4**

PESTO MEATBALL PASTA

500g pork mince
125g mini-mozzarella balls or
  1 large ball, cut into chunks
olive oil
300g dried linguine pasta
100g sunblush tomatoes
sea salt
black pepper

Pesto
50g pine nuts
large handful of fresh basil
1/2 garlic clove
lemon juice, to taste
2 tbsp olive oil
  (more if needed)
30g Parmesan cheese,
  grated, plus extra
  for serving

1 First toast the pine nuts for the pesto in a dry pan for a minute or so. Keep a close eye on them, as they burn easily. Put the pine nuts in a blender with the basil, garlic and lemon juice. Start blending while drizzling in the oil until you have a loose paste. Scoop the pesto into a bowl and stir in the Parmesan cheese.

2 In a large bowl, mix the pork mince with 2 tablespoons of the pesto and season well with salt and pepper. Take a golf ball-sized piece of mixture and flatten it in the palm of your hand. Place a piece of mozzarella on top and mould the pork mixture around the cheese, then add some more mince and shape it into a ball. Repeat until you have used all of the mixture – you should have about 12 meatballs. Cover the meatballs with cling film and chill them in the fridge for about 30 minutes.

3 Heat a non-stick frying pan, add a dash of oil and fry the meatballs for 10–12 minutes until coloured all over and cooked through. Bring a large pan of salted water to the boil for the pasta.

4 Cook the linguine according to the packet instructions. Drain, then stir in the remaining pesto and serve with the meatballs, sunblush tomatoes and some shavings of Parmesan.

Pork and apple is a classic combination – like lamb and mint or beef and horseradish. A few years ago when butchers and supermarkets came up with pork and apple sausages I thought all my dreams had come true! I then took things one step further to make one of my favourite burgers. SERVES 4

PORK AND APPLE BURGERS WITH CELERIAC SLAW

olive oil
1/2 onion, finely diced
1/2 Granny Smith apple,
    diced
400g pork mince
1 tsp fennel seeds
50g fresh breadcrumbs
1 egg, beaten
4 burger buns
1 red onion, sliced,
    for serving (optional)
sea salt
black pepper

Celeriac slaw
1/2 small head celeriac
small squeeze of lemon juice
4 tbsp mayonnaise
40g cornichons, finely
    chopped
1 tbsp chopped flat-leaf
    parsley
2 tbsp Dijon mustard
1/2 Granny Smith apple

1 Heat a dash of oil in a non-stick frying pan and cook the diced onion and apple for 6–7 minutes until softened but not coloured. Remove them from the pan and leave to cool. Once cooled, add the mince, fennel seeds, breadcrumbs and beaten egg, season well and mix everything together. Shape the mixture into 4 patties, cover with cling film and leave them to chill in the fridge for 30 minutes. Preheat the oven to 200°C/180°C Fan/Gas 6.

2 To make the slaw, peel the celeriac and chop it into matchsticks, then dress it with the lemon juice. Add the mayonnaise, cornichons, parsley and mustard and leave the salad to stand for at least 20 minutes. Just before serving, peel the apple half, cut it into matchsticks and stir them into the slaw.

3 Heat an ovenproof pan on the hob, add a little oil and fry the burgers for 4–5 minutes on each side. Transfer the pan to the preheated oven for 5–6 minutes or until the burgers are cooked through. Toast the buns and serve the burgers on them with some slices of red onion, if you like, and the celeriac slaw on the side.

If you're having a picnic or party, these beauties should be the first thing on the menu. I hate dried-out, flavourless, shop-bought sausage rolls, but try tucking into a tasty, moist, home-made version that's packed with flavour and served warm so that the puff pastry is still flaky – amazing! I think you'll see where I'm coming from with this and these are actually really simple to make. Use your favourite sausages, whatever the flavour, and serve with some chutney. MAKES 4

SUPER-EASY SAUSAGE ROLLS

olive oil
1 small onion, finely diced
8 good-quality sausages
1 tbsp fresh thyme (leaves
    picked from the stems),
    plus extra for sprinkling
60g Parmesan cheese, grated
500g pack of puff pastry
flour, for dusting
1 egg, beaten
sea salt
black pepper

1 Warm the oil in a non-stick frying pan and cook the onion for 5–6 minutes until softened. Remove from the pan and leave to cool.

2 Skin the sausages, place the meat in a large bowl and mix in the cooled onion, thyme and cheese. Season with salt and pepper.

3 Roll out the puff pastry on a floured surface to the thickness of a £1 coin. Trim the pastry into a rectangle measuring about 50 x 30cm, then cut this in half. Divide the sausage mixture in 2 and shape each half into rough sausage shapes. Lay 1 sausage shape along 1 half of a piece of pastry. Brush the edge of the pastry with beaten egg, then fold it over the sausage meat. Crimp along the edge with a fork, then trim away any excess pastry. Cut this sausage roll in half, then repeat with the other piece of pastry and filling. Preheat the oven to 200°C/180°C Fan/Gas 6.

4 Lay the sausage rolls on a baking sheet lined with baking parchment and brush the tops with beaten egg. Sprinkle with some fresh thyme. Bake in the preheated oven for 25–30 minutes or until golden and cooked through.

We Bristol boys love our cider. This dish is definitely a winter warmer but much lighter than you would expect from comfort food. Try to get a medium cider as some of the sweeter ones tend to make this cassoulet too sugary. Serving with champ works brilliantly – you need something to mop up the sauce. As the Wurzels would say, ooh arr! SERVES 4

PORK AND CIDER CASSOULET

Meatballs
400g pork mince
1 onion, diced
1 tbsp fresh thyme (leaves picked from the stems)
olive oil
sea salt
black pepper

Sauce
180g smoked, cubed pancetta
1 onion, diced
2 garlic cloves, crushed
250g chestnut mushrooms, wiped and sliced
a few sprigs of thyme
400ml dry cider
300ml chicken stock
1 tbsp crème fraiche
2 tbsp chopped flat-leaf parsley

Champ
800g potatoes, quartered
200ml milk, warmed
small knob of unsalted butter
6 spring onions, sliced

1 In a large bowl, mix the pork mince, onion, and thyme, then season. Roll the mixture into golf ball-sized meatballs, cover with cling film and leave them to chill in the fridge for 20 minutes if you have time. Heat a dash of oil in a non-stick frying pan and cook the meatballs over a medium heat until coloured. Remove them from the pan and set aside.

2 Now make the sauce. Put the pancetta in the pan and cook until golden, then add the onion, garlic, mushrooms and thyme and cook for a few minutes. Pour in the cider, then scrape up any sticky bits from the bottom of the pan. Add the stock and meatballs, then cover the pan with a lid and simmer for 1½ hours over a gentle heat. Before serving, stir in a tablespoon of crème fraiche and the chopped parsley and check the seasoning. Serve with the champ.

3 To make the champ, boil the potatoes in salted water until cooked through. Drain them and mash with the warmed milk and butter until smooth. Season with salt and black pepper, then stir the spring onions into the mash.

Some of my fondest food memories are from my school days, when we ate everything from Scotch eggs and pork stroganoff to Australian crunch with fluorescent green mint custard. School dinners seem to get a bad rep but I loved them. This is my version of the paprika-rich stroganoff I enjoyed as a child. Takes me back to good, good times. Serve with some plain boiled rice. **SERVES 4**

PORK MEATBALL STROGANOFF

500g pork mince
1 tbsp smoked paprika
2 tbsp chopped flat-leaf
  parsley, plus extra
  for serving
2 garlic cloves, crushed
olive oil
150g chestnut mushrooms,
  washed and sliced
1 large onion, sliced
30ml brandy (optional)
150ml crème fraiche
1 tsp Dijon mustard
sea salt
black pepper

1 Sprinkle the mince with some of the paprika, add the parsley and garlic, then season well with salt and pepper. Shape the mixture into small meatballs, then cover with cling film and leave them to chill in the fridge for 20 minutes. Heat a frying pan, add a dash of oil and fry the meatballs for 10–12 minutes or until cooked through. Remove them from the pan and set aside.

2 Add a little more oil to the pan and fry the mushrooms for 5–6 minutes until golden. Reduce the heat, add the onion and cook for another 5 minutes. Pour in the brandy, if using, and cook until the liquid has nearly evaporated. Stir in the crème fraiche, mustard and remaining paprika, then put the meatballs back into the pan. Simmer for 3–4 minutes and then serve with a garnish of flat-leaf parsley.

A good Thai curry balances four flavours – hot, sweet, salty and sour – for a perfect combination by anyone's standards. If you want a slightly quicker version of this recipe, you can get very good Thai curry pastes in supermarkets and Asian food stores. Serve with a portion of fragrant jasmine rice (see p. 199). SERVES 4

PORK MEATBALL THAI CURRY

500g pork mince
1 tsp ground coriander
olive oil
1 onion, sliced
1 stick of lemon grass
1 x 400g can of coconut milk
150ml chicken stock
1 tbsp nam pla (fish sauce)
150g baby asparagus
1 lime
1 tbsp sugar
3 tbsp chopped fresh
    coriander, for serving
sea salt
black pepper

Thai paste
1 onion, peeled and
    roughly chopped
4 garlic cloves, peeled
1 thumb-sized piece of
    fresh root ginger, peeled
1 red chilli, deseeded
    and chopped
1 tbsp oil

1 In a mini blender, blitz the ingredients for the Thai paste until smooth and set aside.

2 In a bowl, mix the mince and ground coriander with some seasoning. Shape the mixture into golf ball-sized meatballs, then cover with cling film and leave them to chill in the fridge for 30 minutes. Heat a little oil in a non-stick pan and fry the meatballs until golden, then set them aside.

3 Fry the sliced onion for 5 minutes until softened, then add your Thai paste and lemon grass – bruise the lemon grass first by bashing it with a rolling pin. Continue to cook for a couple of minutes, then pour in the coconut milk, stock and fish sauce and bring to a gentle simmer.

4 Add the meatballs to the pan and cook for 10 minutes, then add the asparagus and cook for another 5 minutes. Add a good squeeze of lime juice and the sugar to balance the flavours in the dish, then taste and add more lime or sugar if you like. Stir in the fresh coriander before serving.

Pasta is a firm favourite in my home, especially when time is at a premium. Sometimes, after a long day at work, a simple, tasty, quick dish like this is just right. Use whatever sausages you like, but try to buy good-quality ones with a high meat content. My favourite for this is the 'Lucifer' from a sausage maker in Bristol – so good but soooo hot! SERVES 4

SAUSAGE AND FIERY TOMATO RIGATONI

6 good-quality pork sausages
olive oil
1 red onion, very finely diced
2 garlic cloves, crushed
1 tbsp fresh thyme (leaves
   picked from the stems)
1 x 400g can of chopped
   tomatoes
1 tsp chilli powder (or to taste)
1 tsp sugar
500g rigatoni pasta
50g Parmesan cheese,
   grated, for serving
sea salt
black pepper

1 Skin the sausages, then divide each of them into 4 small meatballs. Heat a little oil in a non-stick pan and fry the meatballs for 10–12 minutes until golden and cooked through, turning frequently. Remove them from the pan and set aside.

2 Add the diced onion to the pan and fry for 3–4 minutes, then add the garlic and thyme and cook over a medium heat for another 2 minutes. Next add the tomatoes and chilli powder and simmer for 5 minutes. Season with salt and pepper and the sugar.

3 Cook the rigatoni in boiling salted water according to the packet instructions. Drain the pasta and add it to the sauce with the meatballs. Serve with plenty of grated Parmesan cheese.

Laksa is a fragrant noodle-based broth from Malaysia and adding the minced pork gives it extra body. You'll find vermicelli rice noodles in many supermarkets or in Asian grocery stores, but you could use egg noodles instead. **SERVES 4**

SPICY PORK AND BUTTERNUT LAKSA

1 small butternut squash, peeled and cubed
olive oil
350g pork mince
1 thumb-sized piece of fresh root ginger, peeled
1 red chilli, plus extra sliced chilli for garnish
3 garlic cloves, peeled
1 onion, roughly chopped
1 tsp brown sugar
1 x 400ml can of coconut milk
700ml chicken stock
400g vermicelli rice noodles
100g beansprouts
2 tbsp soy sauce
juice of 1/2 lime
3 tbsp chopped fresh coriander
30g salted peanuts, for serving
lime wedges, for serving
sea salt
black pepper

1 Preheat the oven to 200°C/180°C Fan/Gas 6. Place the squash cubes on a baking tray, drizzle them with olive oil and season with salt and pepper. Roast the squash in the preheated oven for about 45 minutes.

2 Heat a dash of oil in a non-stick frying pan and brown the pork mince over a high heat for 5–6 minutes. Remove and set aside.

3 Put the ginger, chilli, garlic, onion and sugar in a small blender and blitz to a paste. Add a little more oil to the frying pan and fry the paste for 2–3 minutes. Pour in the coconut milk and stock, then bring to the boil. Reduce the heat to a simmer, add the pork and roasted butternut squash, then cook gently for 15–20 minutes.

4 Meanwhile, cook the noodles. Bring a pan of salted water to the boil. Add the noodles, turn off the heat and leave them for 5 minutes. Drain, then divide the noodles between 4 bowls.

5 Just before serving, add the beansprouts to the pan with the pork and coconut milk to warm through, then season with soy sauce and lime juice to taste. Ladle the liquid, pork and squash on top of the noodles, then garnish with fresh coriander, peanuts and sliced chilli. Serve with lime wedges to squeeze over the laksa.

This is the dish I make when I crave something sweet and sour. Times have changed, but when I was growing up it was a real treat for us to get a Chinese takeaway, and fried rice with extra peas was always at the top of my list. I remember asking to go to a Chinese restaurant for my thirteenth birthday – even then I was mad about food. Try to cook the rice ahead of time so it has time to chill. **SERVES 4**

STICKY LEMON PORK WITH FRIED RICE

olive oil
400g pork mince
2 garlic cloves, crushed
juice and grated zest
 of 1 lemon
2 tbsp honey
1 tbsp soy sauce
½ red chilli, thinly sliced
1 tbsp chopped fresh
 coriander, for garnish

Fried rice and peas
300g brown basmati rice
olive oil
100g shelled raw prawns
100g frozen peas, defrosted
2 eggs, beaten
soy sauce
4 spring onions, finely sliced

1 Put the rice in a pan with double the volume of water. Bring to the boil, then cover, turn down the heat and cook for about 30 minutes or until tender. Drain and cool as quickly as you can.

2 Heat a frying pan, add a dash of oil and fry the pork mince for 8–10 minutes. Add the garlic and cook for 1 minute, then add the lemon juice and zest, honey, soy sauce and chilli. Tip the mixture into a serving bowl and sprinkle with coriander.

3 Add a little more oil to the frying pan. Fry the prawns for 2–3 minutes, then add the rice and peas and continue cooking for 3–4 minutes. Add the beaten eggs, stirring so the egg breaks up and coats the rice, then a splash of soy sauce. Finally, stir in the spring onions before serving the rice and peas with the pork.

If you need an idea for a light supper, give this one a whirl. There's not much cooking involved, but the results are so good. You can buy sweet chilli sauce, of course, but it's so easy to make your own. Use what you need for this recipe, then put the rest in a bowl in the fridge to enjoy another time. SERVES 4

SWEET CHILLI PORK WITH RICE NOODLES

olive oil
400g pork mince
1 small piece of fresh root
   ginger, peeled and cut
   into matchsticks
2 garlic cloves, finely sliced
2 tbsp soy sauce
juice of ½ lime
200g vermicelli rice noodles
1 carrot, cut into matchsticks
3 spring onions, cut into
   matchsticks
1 tbsp chopped fresh
   coriander, for garnish
lime wedges, for serving
   (optional)

Sweet chilli sauce
3 red chillies, roughly
   chopped
3 garlic cloves, peeled
1 tbsp soy sauce
80g caster sugar
80ml cider vinegar
50ml water

1 First make the sweet chilli sauce. Put all the ingredients in a blender and whizz until smooth. Pour the mixture into a saucepan and bring to the boil, then lower the heat and reduce until the sauce is syrupy. Set aside to cool.

2 Heat some oil in a frying pan and fry the pork mince for 10–12 minutes until golden and cooked through. Add the ginger, garlic, soy sauce and 3 tablespoons of the sweet chilli sauce. Stir to combine, then add the lime juice to taste.

3 When the pork is nearly ready, place the noodles in a bowl and cover them with boiling water. Leave them to soak for 5 minutes, then drain well.

4 Serve the mince on top of the noodles and scatter over the carrot, spring onions and coriander. Add some lime wedges on the side for squeezing over the dish if you like.

Patatas bravas is a famous Spanish dish, usually served in small portions as tapas. It's so good, I think it deserves to stand alone as a main meal of crispy fried potatoes, topped with some beautiful pork and chorizo meatballs braised in a rich and spicy tomato sauce. I sometimes grate Manchego cheese over the top before serving. If you prefer, you could roast the parboiled potatoes in a hot oven until crispy instead of frying them. Serve with a courgette ribbon salad (see p. 200) SERVES 4

PORK AND CHORIZO PATATAS BRAVAS

Meatballs
500g pork mince
100g uncured chorizo
  sausages, skinned
1/2 red onion
1/2 tsp smoked paprika
30g fresh breadcrumbs
1 tbsp chopped flat-leaf
  parsley
olive oil
sea salt
black pepper

Patatas bravas
olive oil
1 red onion, finely diced
2 garlic cloves, crushed
1/2 red chilli, finely diced
100ml red wine
1/2 tsp smoked paprika
1 x 400g can of chopped
  tomatoes
200ml chicken stock
1 tsp sugar
600g Maris Piper potatoes
2 tbsp chopped flat-leaf
  parsley

1 Mix the mince, chorizo, onion, paprika, breadcrumbs and parsley in a bowl and season. Roll the mixture into about 16 golf ball-sized meatballs, cover with cling film and leave them to chill in the fridge for 20 minutes if you have time. Heat a little oil in a frying pan and cook the meatballs over a medium heat until coloured. Remove them and set aside.

2 Now start the sauce for the patatas bravas. Place a saucepan over a medium heat, add a dash of oil and fry the onion, garlic and chilli for 5 minutes until softened. Pour in the wine and cook until the liquid has reduced by half. Add the paprika, tomatoes and stock, then bring the sauce to a simmer. Add the meatballs and cook for 20 minutes, then add the sugar and season.

3 Meanwhile, prepare the potatoes. Peel the potatoes and cut them into 2cm cubes. Bring a pan of salted water to the boil, add the potatoes and cook for 5 minutes. Drain them and leave to dry out for 5 minutes. Heat some olive oil in the frying pan and fry the potatoes until golden and crispy. This will take 10–15 minutes.

4 To serve, spoon the meatballs and sauce over the potatoes and sprinkle with parsley.

I'm guessing that at one time or another you may have paid a visit to a certain Scandinavian superstore. You may have ventured into the café and ordered some of the fairly anaemic-looking meatballs with pallid gravy – and like me, you loved them! They're one of my guilty pleasures and here is my version. As you are using a combo of pork and beef mince, this recipe makes a double quantity of the meatballs so freeze half and use them within a month. Serve with some mashed potatoes (see p. 195) and a spoonful of lingonberry or cranberry sauce. SERVES 4

SCANDINAVIAN MEATBALL SPECIAL

olive oil
2 onions, grated
500g pork mince
500g beef mince
30g fresh breadcrumbs
2 eggs, beaten
a few gratings of nutmeg
sea salt
black pepper

Gravy
20g unsalted butter
1 shallot, finely diced
1 garlic clove, crushed
1 tsp flour
200ml beef stock
150ml soured cream
2 tbsp chopped fresh chives

1 Heat a non-stick frying pan, add a dash of oil and cook the onions for 5–6 minutes. Leave to cool. Put the mince in a bowl and add the cooled onions, breadcrumbs, eggs and nutmeg, then season with salt and pepper. Roll the mixture into small meatballs, cover them with cling film and chill in the fridge for 20 minutes. Unless you want to cook them all, you can freeze half the meatballs at this point.

2 Add a little more oil to the frying pan and fry the meatballs for 10–12 minutes until golden all over, then set them aside.

3 To make the gravy, add the butter to the pan and gently cook the shallot and garlic for 2–3 minutes. Stir in the flour and cook for another minute, then add the stock and simmer for a few minutes. Stir in the soured cream and chives, then put the meatballs back in the pan to warm through before serving.

The Italians call the mixture of veg that forms the base of their meatballs *soffritto*. This is the holy trinity of onion, carrot and celery and you will not believe how much flavour this simple combo will add to your meatballs. I know it might seem a bit of a faff, but believe me it's worth it. This great family pasta dish reminds me of the sort of thing you see in the old Mafia movies when *mamma* brings out a giant platter of food and everyone helps themselves. Serve with lots of garlic bread. SERVES 4

TOMATO AND MEATBALL PASTA

olive oil
1 small onion, finely diced
1 small carrot, very finely diced
1 celery stick, finely diced
3 garlic cloves, crushed
500g pork mince
1 tsp dried chilli flakes
100ml buttermilk
40g Parmesan cheese, grated
60g fresh breadcrumbs
500g dried linguine pasta
30g Parmesan cheese,
 cut into shavings
2 tbsp chopped flat-leaf
 parsley
sea salt
black pepper

Sauce
100g smoked, cubed pancetta
1 red onion, very finely diced
3 garlic cloves, crushed
1 tbsp very finely chopped
 fresh rosemary
500ml passata
1 tsp chilli powder (or to taste)
1 tsp sugar

1 Heat a non-stick pan, add a dash of oil and cook the onion, carrot, celery and garlic for about 10 minutes. Leave to cool. Put the mince in a bowl and add the cooked veg, chilli, buttermilk, cheese and breadcrumbs. Season with salt and pepper, then mould the mixture into about 16 meatballs. Put them on a plate, cover with cling film and chill in the fridge for 20 minutes.

2 Add a dash more oil to the pan and fry the meatballs for about 7–8 minutes until coloured, then set aside. Do this in batches if necessary, so you don't overcrowd the pan.

3 Using the same pan, fry the pancetta for the sauce until golden, then add the onion, garlic and rosemary and cook over a medium heat for a further 3 minutes. Add the passata and chilli powder, then put the meatballs back in the pan. Simmer for 15–20 minutes or until the meatballs are cooked through, then season with salt and pepper and the sugar.

4 Meanwhile, bring a pan of salted water to the boil and cook the linguine according to the packet instructions. Drain, then add the pasta to the meatballs and tomato sauce. Stir the sauce through the pasta and serve with Parmesan shavings and flat-leaf parsley.

The great thing about these wraps is that you can serve them as a main meal or as brilliant canapés when you have friends round. Ketjap manis is a sweet Indonesian soy sauce but if you can't find it, use a good-quality soy sauce with a teaspoon of brown sugar. Quick to cook, this is an amazing dish for warm summer nights. SERVES 4

VIETNAMESE PORK LETTUCE WRAPS

olive oil
500g pork mince
1 small onion, diced
2 garlic cloves, crushed
1/2 red chilli, deseeded and
    sliced, plus extra to garnish
1 tbsp grated fresh root ginger
2 tbsp ketjap manis
1 tsp sweet chilli sauce
juice of 1/2 lime
2 baby gem lettuces
1 tbsp chopped fresh mint
1 tbsp chopped fresh
    coriander, to garnish

Pickled carrot
1 small carrot, cut into
    matchsticks
1 small onion, finely sliced
1 tsp salt
3 spring onions, finely sliced
1 garlic clove, crushed
1 green chilli, deseeded
    and finely chopped
juice of 1 lemon
1 tsp sugar

1 Heat a non-stick frying pan, add a dash of oil and cook the pork mince for 7–8 minutes, breaking it up as it cooks. Throw in the onion, garlic, chilli and ginger and cook for 3–4 minutes longer. Pour in the ketjap manis and sweet chilli sauce, turn off the heat, then add the lime juice.

2 To make the pickled carrot, put the carrots and onion in a bowl, then sprinkle on the salt and leave for 10 minutes. Drain off any excess liquid, then add the rest of the ingredients. Leave to marinate for 10 minutes before serving.

3 Separate the lettuce leaves from the baby gem lettuce and spoon some of the mince mixture into each one. Add some fresh mint and garnish with coriander and extra chilli if you like, then top with some pickled carrot.

This fantastic Moroccan summer tagine is light and fresh, with a zingy lemon taste. I've bulked this recipe out with a can of chickpeas, something I always keep in my store cupboard, not just for tagines but for curries and pasta dishes too! Serve with some fruity couscous (see p. 198) and flatbreads. SERVES 4

FRUITY PORK AND OLIVE TAGINE

500g pork mince
½ onion, finely diced
30g dried apricots, chopped
40g fresh breadcrumbs
grated zest of ½ lemon
small squeeze of lemon juice
olive oil
sea salt
black pepper

Sauce
olive oil
1 large onion, finely chopped
3 garlic cloves, crushed
1 thumb-sized piece of fresh
   root ginger, peeled
   and grated
1 tsp smoked paprika
1 tsp ground cinnamon
1 tsp ground cumin
1 x 400g can of chopped
   tomatoes
1 x 400g can of chickpeas
grated zest of ½ lemon
40g dried apricots, chopped
140ml chicken stock
1 tbsp honey
50g pitted green olives
handful of flaked almonds

1 Mix the pork mince, diced onion, dried apricots, breadcrumbs, lemon zest and juice in a bowl, then season with salt and pepper. Shape the mixture into golf ball-sized meatballs, then cover with cling film and chill in the fridge for 30 minutes. Heat a little oil in a non-stick frying pan and fry the meatballs for 6–7 minutes until coloured. Remove them from the pan and set aside while you make the sauce.

2 Heat a dash of oil in a large saucepan – you need one with a lid – and fry the onion, garlic and ginger until softened. Add the spices and cook for 1–2 minutes, then add the tomatoes, chickpeas, lemon zest and chopped apricots. Add the meatballs, pour in the stock, then cover the pan with a lid and cook for 1 hour over a low heat.

3 Just before serving, add the honey, olives and season with salt and pepper. Scatter over the flaked almonds for extra crunch.

Home-made Scotch eggs are in a different league from shop-bought. I love using chorizo-style sausages for this recipe, but any good-quality sausage meat is fine, so try pork and apple or your favourite banger from your local butcher. As always, be very careful when deep frying and never leave your pan of hot oil unattended. **SERVES 4**

SCORCHING CHORIZO SCOTCH EGGS

6 medium free-range eggs
2 tbsp plain flour, plus extra
  for dusting
300g pork and chorizo
  sausages
20g Parmesan cheese, grated
1 tsp fresh thyme (leaves
  picked from the stems)
80g dry breadcrumbs
vegetable oil, for deep frying

1 Place 4 of the eggs in a saucepan and cover them with cold water. Bring the water to the boil over a high heat, then turn off the heat and leave for 3 minutes. Immediately place the eggs into cold water to stop the cooking process. Change the water a few times before peeling. Dry the peeled eggs gently, then dust them with flour.

2 Skin the sausages, put the sausage meat in a bowl, then mix in the cheese and thyme. Divide the mixture into 4 and roll into balls. Take 1 ball, put it on top of a piece of cling film, then roll it out until it is about 5mm thick. Place 1 of the eggs in the centre of the sausage meat, then using the cling film bring up the sides, pull away the film and gently mould the meat around the egg until it is completely enclosed. Repeat with the rest of the sausage meat and eggs.

3 Beat the other 2 eggs in a bowl and put the flour and breadcrumbs in separate bowls. One at a time, dip the Scotch eggs into the flour, then the egg and lastly the breadcrumbs, making sure they are completely coated. Cover with cling film and chill them in the fridge for 20 minutes.

4 Fill a large saucepan one-third full with vegetable oil and heat to 170°C. Test the temperature with a piece of bread – if it turns golden in a minute, the oil is hot enough. Deep fry the eggs for 4–5 minutes, then drain on kitchen paper. Serve immediately with some ketchup and mustard.

It seems like nearly every American movie I watched when growing up had a scene where the family sat round the table and ate a home-cooked meatloaf. I cannot understand why this dish has not caught on over here in the same way. It's substantial, tasty and economical so it ticks all the boxes for good family cooking. I like to eat mine with gravy, asparagus and perhaps some sauté potatoes (see p. 196). SERVES 4

BAKED YANKEE MEATLOAF

100g smoked, cubed pancetta
1 onion, finely diced
1 large carrot, finely diced
2 celery sticks, finely diced
200g pork mince
400g beef mince
1 tbsp fresh thyme (leaves
    picked from the stems)
2 eggs, beaten
olive oil, for greasing
8–10 rashers of streaky bacon
sea salt
black pepper

1 Fry the pancetta in a dry frying pan until it starts to turn golden, then add the onion, carrot and celery. Cook them gently over a medium heat for 8–10 minutes, then leave to cool.

2 Put the mince in a bowl, add the cooked veg and pancetta, then stir in the thyme and eggs. Season with salt and pepper and mix well. Preheat the oven to 200°C/180°C Fan/Gas 6.

3 Grease a 450g loaf tin with oil, then line it with rashers of streaky bacon. Spoon the meatloaf mixture into the tin, cover with foil, then place the tin on a baking tray. Pour boiling water from a kettle into the baking tray until it comes about halfway up the sides of the loaf tin. Bake in the preheated oven for 40 minutes.

4 Take the meatloaf out of the oven and remove the foil. Turn up the heat to 220°C/200°C Fan/Gas 7. Pour off any juices from the tin, then put the meatfloaf back in the oven to brown for 15–20 minutes. Leave the meatloaf to rest for 5 minutes before turning out and serving.

You won't find any of the scary ingredients associated with a traditional faggot recipe in my version. Think of them as giant meatballs, seasoned with sage and thyme and cooked gently in a rich onion gravy. My faggots aren't wrapped in caul fat so you will definitely need to chill them for a good half an hour to firm them up before flouring and searing them in a hot pan. Serve with mash (see p. 195), spiked with wholegrain mustard. SERVES 4

BRAISED FAGGOTS WITH RICH ONION GRAVY

olive oil
1 onion, diced
400g pork mince
400g beef mince
1 tbsp finely chopped
   fresh sage
1 tbsp fresh thyme (leaves
   picked from the stems)
½ tsp mace
1 egg, beaten
40g dry breadcrumbs
30g plain flour, for dusting
sea salt
black pepper

Rich onion gravy
2 red onions, sliced
2 garlic cloves, crushed
2-3 sprigs of fresh thyme
1 tbsp plain flour
300ml red wine
800ml beef stock
1 tbsp redcurrant jelly

1 Heat a little oil in a non-stick ovenproof pan that has a lid. Fry the diced onion for 5-6 minutes over a medium heat, then tip it into a bowl and leave to cool. Set the pan aside for later. Add the mince, sage, thyme, mace, egg and breadcrumbs to the cooled onion, then season with salt and pepper. Mix until the ingredients come together, but don't overwork. Divide the mixture into 12, then shape into balls, cover with cling film and put them in the fridge to chill for 30 minutes.

2 Heat a dash more oil in the pan you used for the onions. Dust the faggots with flour, then seal them all over in the hot pan. This will take 5-7 minutes and you may need to cook the faggots in batches, depending on the size of your pan. Set the faggots aside once sealed. Preheat the oven to 190°C/170°C Fan/Gas 5.

3 Now make the gravy. Put the sliced red onions into the pan and cook for 7-8 minutes until they are softened, then add the garlic and thyme. Cook for a further minute, then stir in the flour. Pour in the wine and stock and bring the gravy to the boil before seasoning with salt and pepper. Finally, stir in the redcurrant jelly. Add the faggots to the pan, cover with a lid and place in the preheated oven to cook for 45-50 minutes.

CHAPTER 4

CHICKEN AND TURKEY MINCE

The great thing about the recipes in this chapter is that you can use chicken or turkey in most cases so if you cannot find chicken mince, then grab yourself some turkey instead. Many butchers don't like to mince chicken, as it takes them a while to clean down the mincer afterwards, but I find that pulsing skinless, boneless thighs for a few seconds in a food processor gives excellent results.

Turkey mince is very low in fat. Most supermarkets have two types – thigh meat, which is lean, and breast meat, which is very lean. Both can dry out quite easily so be careful not to overcook them. Turkey mince is also very cheap so is perfect for cooking healthy food on a tight budget. It's great value in my opinion.

The inspiration for this recipe comes from a wonderfully light but tasty jerk chicken pasta I ate while on holiday in Florida. When I came home I started trying to recreate what I had eaten and I reckon this is pretty damn close. I use chicken, but turkey mince would work well too. You can buy jerk pastes in most supermarkets now and some can be quite fiery so watch out. Serve with garlic bread and ice-cold lager. SERVES 4

CARIBBEAN MEATBALL PASTA

1 small onion, finely chopped
2 garlic cloves, crushed
1 tbsp fresh thyme (leaves picked from the stems)
1 small piece of fresh root ginger, peeled and grated
1 tbsp jerk paste
juice of 1/2 lime
400g chicken thighs, skinless and boneless
60g fresh breadcrumbs
olive oil
400g tagliatelle pasta (fresh or dried)
2 handfuls of rocket leaves
80g sunblush tomatoes
sea salt
black pepper

Sauce
olive oil
1 red onion, diced
1/2 red chilli, diced
2 garlic cloves, crushed
150ml white wine
2 tbsp crème fraiche
1/2 lime

1 Put the finely chopped onion, garlic, thyme, ginger, jerk paste and lime juice in a food processor and blitz until broken down. Add the chicken thighs and pulse for a few seconds – it's good to have a few slightly larger pieces of chicken in the mixture.

2 Tip the chicken mixture into a large bowl and mix in the breadcrumbs, then season well. Shape the mixture into golf ball-sized meatballs, then put them on a plate, cover with cling film and chill in the fridge for 30 minutes. Heat a non-stick frying pan, add a dash of oil, then cook the meatballs over a medium heat for 15–17 minutes or until coloured all over and cooked through. Remove and set aside.

3 To make the sauce, add a little more oil to the frying pan and cook the diced red onion, chilli and garlic in a pan for 3–4 minutes until softened. Add the wine and continue to cook until the liquid is reduced by half, then stir in the crème fraiche and a good squeeze of lime juice. Add the meatballs to the pan with the rocket and stir.

4 Bring a large saucepan of salted water to the boil and cook the pasta according to the packet instructions. Drain. Add the pasta and sunblush tomatoes to the pan with the meatballs and toss everything together before serving.

This is a Spanish take on a classic Italian dish – lynch me if you like, but you really should give this a go. You can use turkey or pork mince in this recipe too if you want to skip mincing the chicken thighs. Lovely served with a crisp side salad and some garlic bread. **SERVES 4**

CHICKEN AND CHORIZO LASAGNE

4–5 chicken thighs, skinless and boneless
olive oil
100g chorizo, cubed
1 large onion, very finely diced
2 celery sticks, very finely diced
1 tbsp chopped thyme (leaves picked from the stems)
3 garlic cloves, crushed
150ml white wine
½ tsp smoked paprika
2 x 400g cans of chopped tomatoes
1 tsp sugar
fresh lasagne pasta (about 9 sheets)
70g Cheddar cheese, grated
sea salt
black pepper

White sauce
50g unsalted butter
50g plain flour
500ml milk

1 Put the chicken thighs in a food processor and pulse until they are broken down. Don't over process though, as it's nice to have a few slightly larger pieces in the mixture. Add a dash of oil to a non-stick frying pan, tip in the chicken mince and brown over a medium to high heat. Remove the chicken from the pan and set aside.

2 Using the same pan with a little more oil if you need it, cook the chorizo, onion, celery, thyme and garlic for 5 minutes until softened. Add the wine and continue to cook until the liquid is reduced by half. Put the chicken back in the pan and add the paprika and tomatoes, then reduce the heat to a simmer and cook for 20 minutes. Season with the sugar and salt and pepper.

3 To make the white sauce, melt the butter over a medium heat. Whisk in the flour and cook for 2 minutes, stirring constantly. Pour in the milk and continue whisking until it comes to a boil, then reduce the heat and simmer the sauce for 5 minutes, stirring occasionally, then season.

4 Preheat the oven to 200°C/180°C Fan/Gas 6. Grease an ovenproof dish measuring about 33 x 23cm. Spread a thin layer of chicken sauce in the bottom of the dish, then add a sheet of lasagne, then more chicken sauce. Add another sheet of pasta, followed by white sauce, then the chicken sauce. Continue until everything is used up, finishing with a layer of white sauce. Sprinkle with cheese and bake in the oven for 40 minutes.

Punchy and packed full of some beautiful Indonesian flavours, this is a great supper dish and you can use leftover rice if you have any. I like to use brown basmati rice, as the grains stay beautifully separate when cooked and don't become stodgy. SERVES 4

CHICKEN NASI GORENG

400g brown basmati rice
olive oil
400g chicken mince
   (or use 4–5 chicken
   thighs – see p. 137)
4 shallots, peeled
3 garlic cloves, peeled
1 red chilli
1 tbsp brown sugar
1 tbsp tomato purée
2 tbsp soy sauce
3 spring onions, finely sliced
2 tbsp fresh chopped
   coriander
2 eggs
20g salted peanuts
1/2 cucumber, deseeded
   and cut into batons
sea salt
black pepper

1 Put the rice in a saucepan and add double the volume of cold water. Bring to the boil, then turn the heat down low, cover the pan and cook for 25–30 minutes.

2 Heat a large wok-type pan or non-stick frying pan, add a dash of oil and fry the chicken mince for 5–6 minutes or until browned.

3 Put 2 of the shallots into a food processor, add the garlic, chilli, sugar, tomato purée and soy sauce, then blend until smooth. Chop the remaining 2 shallots and add them to the pan with the chicken, then tip in the shallot purée. Cook for a couple of minutes, add the cooked rice and fry for 4–5 minutes until heated through. Sprinkle on the spring onions and coriander.

4 Beat the eggs and season them with salt and pepper. Heat a dash of oil in a medium-sized non-stick frying pan and add the eggs. Roll the pan around so the eggs coat the base in a thin layer and cook for 1–2 minutes. Turn and cook the eggs on the other side for a further minute. Remove the egg pancake from the pan, roll it up and slice. Serve the nasi goreng garnished with peanuts, cucumber and slices of egg pancake.

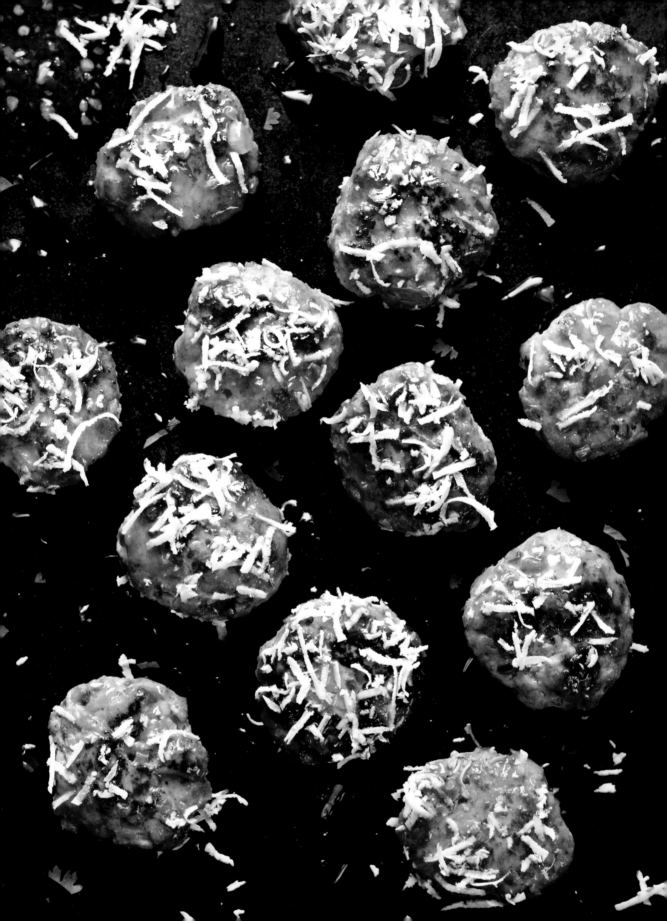

I love this dish. I've always been a sucker for a peanut-rich satay sauce and order it whenever I see it on a menu. This dish has all the elements you're looking for in Asian food − hot, sweet, salty and sour − and this is why it works so well. If you don't like too much heat, then switch the sweet chilli sauce for honey. **SERVES 4**

COCONUT CHICKEN PATTIES WITH SATAY SAUCE

½ onion, peeled and finely
    chopped
3 garlic cloves, crushed
1 heaped tbsp red Thai
    curry paste
40g breadcrumbs
1 tbsp soy sauce
juice of 1 lime
2 tbsp chopped fresh
    coriander
500g chicken or turkey mince
olive oil
2 tbsp sweet chilli sauce
1 pack of fresh coconut
    pieces, flesh grated

Satay sauce
olive oil
½ onion, finely sliced
1 garlic clove, crushed
½ red chilli, deseeded
100g crunchy peanut butter
juice of 1 lime
1 tbsp muscovado sugar
1 tbsp soy sauce
100ml coconut milk

1 Mix the chopped onion, garlic, curry paste, breadcrumbs, soy sauce, lime juice and coriander in a large bowl until well combined. Mix in the chicken or turkey mince and then shape the mixture into 8 balls. I like to then flatten the balls so they resemble patties or mini burgers. Cover them with cling film and leave in the fridge to chill for 20 minutes.

2 To make the satay sauce, heat a little oil in a small saucepan and fry the onion, garlic and chilli for 3–4 minutes until softened. Add the rest of the ingredients to the pan and cook the sauce for a further 5 minutes.

3 Heat a non-stick pan, add a dash of oil and cook the patties for 5–6 minutes on each side. Once the patties are cooked through, brush them with the sweet chilli sauce, then sprinkle on the grated coconut to coat the outsides. Serve with the satay sauce.

If you like Chinese food you're almost sure to have tried the famous duck pancakes. I always eat too many and don't leave enough room for the rest of the meal – they are that good! Try my version using minced chicken thighs, but you can use turkey mince if you like. **SERVES 4**

FIVE-SPICE CHICKEN PANCAKES

400g chicken thighs, boneless
    and skinless (or use 4–5
    chicken thighs – see p. 137)
olive oil
2 garlic cloves, crushed
1/2 red chilli, sliced (optional)
1 tsp Chinese five-spice
    powder
2 tbsp hoisin sauce,
    plus extra for serving
1 tbsp soy sauce
12 Chinese pancakes
    (available in supermarkets
    and Asian groceries)
6 spring onions, thinly sliced
1/2 cucumber, cut into batons
bunch of chives

1 Put the chicken thighs in a food processor and blitz for 5–6 seconds. Don't overprocess – it's good to have some texture. Heat a dash of oil in a non-stick frying pan and fry the chicken for 4–5 minutes. Add the garlic, chilli and spice and continue cooking for 2–3 minutes or until the chicken is cooked through. Stir in the hoisin and soy sauce.

2 Warm the pancakes in a microwave or in a bamboo steamer if you have one. To eat, spread a smear of hoisin sauce on a warmed pancake, then top with some chicken. Add a generous helping of spring onions and cucumber, then roll up the pancake. Tie it with some chives if you like, and enjoy. Simple as that!

I wasn't too keen on courgettes, but then I was introduced to the delights of them cooked with garlic and butter until soft and sticky. This is a simple, tasty meal that everyone will love. If you can get some fresh oregano, sprinkle some leaves over the courgettes before serving. **SERVES 4**

STUFFED COURGETTE MELT

4 large courgettes
olive oil
40g pine nuts
300g chicken mince
   (or use 3–4 chicken
   thighs – see p. 137)
4 garlic cloves, crushed
½ onion, very finely diced
20g unsalted butter
2 tbsp cream cheese
60g feta cheese, crumbled
50g Parmesan cheese, grated
30g breadcrumbs
1 tbsp fresh oregano
   (optional)
1 lemon, quartered,
   for serving
sea salt
black pepper

1 Preheat the oven to 210°C/190°C Fan/Gas 6½. Cut the courgettes in half lengthways, then scoop out some of the flesh from the centres. Dice the scooped-out flesh and set it aside. Place the halves on a baking tray, drizzle them with a little olive oil and season with salt and pepper, then roast for 15 minutes in the preheated oven. Toast the pine nuts by putting them in a dry pan over a medium heat for a couple of minutes. Shake the pan and keep a close eye on the pine nuts – they burn all too easily.

2 While the courgettes are roasting, brown the chicken mince in a dash of oil in a frying pan for 3–4 minutes. Add the diced courgette flesh, garlic, onion and butter, cook for a further 5 minutes, then season. Take the pan off the heat and stir in the pine nuts and cream cheese.

3 Take the courgettes out of the oven and fill them with the chicken mixture. Sprinkle the crumbled feta, Parmesan and breadcrumbs on top, then put the courgettes back in the oven for 10–12 minutes or until the cheese has melted. Sprinkle with the oregano, if using, and serve with the lemon quarters for squeezing.

These Spanish-inspired burgers are a hit every time I make them. The flavours are strong but they all work together to make this one of my absolute favourite burgers. If you cannot find chorizo-style pork sausages, with the same texture as normal sausages, chop up some semi-cured chorizo and add that to the mince instead. Peppadew are small, sweet, slightly spicy peppers and you'll find them in the deli aisle at the supermarket. I also like to eat them on pizzas or stuffed with a little cream cheese. **SERVES 4**

CHICKEN AND CHORIZO BURGERS

200g chicken mince
 (or use 2–3 chicken
 thighs – see p. 137)
3 chorizo-style pork
 sausages, skinned
1 shallot, finely chopped
2 garlic cloves, crushed
40g pitted green olives,
 chopped
1 tbsp fresh thyme (leaves
 picked from the stems)
60g fresh breadcrumbs
olive oil
4 slices of Manchego cheese
4 rustic buns
black pepper

Smoky paprika mayo
3 tbsp mayonnaise
5 Peppadew peppers,
 drained and chopped
1/2 tsp smoked paprika
small squeeze of lemon juice

1 In a large bowl, mix the chicken, sausage meat, shallot, garlic, olives, thyme and breadcrumbs. You probably won't want any additional salt as the olives will be salty but a twist of pepper will be needed. Divide the mixture into 4, then shape into burgers, cover with cling film and chill in the fridge for 30 minutes. Preheat the oven to 200°C/180°C Fan/Gas 6.

2 Heat a little oil in an ovenproof pan on the hob and cook the burgers for 3–4 minutes on each side. Then place them in the preheated oven for 8–10 minutes or until cooked through. A couple of minutes before the end of the cooking time, put a slice of cheese on top of each burger and put them back in the oven.

3 Mix the mayonnaise with the peppers, paprika and lemon juice and keep it in the fridge until needed. Toast the buns and serve the burgers with lashings of smoky paprika mayo.

Mexican or Tex-Mex food has become very popular in Britain and dishes such as fajitas hold a regular place on our tables. Enchiladas are almost like a Mexican take on cannelloni and my chicken version with rich barbecue sauce is a recipe you will keep revisiting. I like these with a big dollop of soured cream. SERVES 4

BBQ CHICKEN ENCHILADAS

olive oil
500g chicken mince
   (or use 5-6 chicken
   thighs – see p. 137)
1 large onion, finely chopped
3 garlic cloves, crushed
1 green pepper, diced
1 x 400g can of red kidney
   beans, drained and rinsed
100ml tomato ketchup
3 tbsp cider vinegar
2 tbsp dark brown sugar
1 tbsp soy sauce
1 tsp English mustard
150ml chicken stock
½ tsp smoked paprika
2 tbsp chopped fresh
   coriander
4 large soft flour tortillas
150g Cheddar cheese, grated
soured cream, for serving
   (optional)
sea salt
black pepper

1 Heat a dash of oil in a non-stick frying pan, add the chicken mince and cook for 4–5 minutes, stirring regularly. Add the onion, garlic and green pepper, then continue to cook for about 5 minutes until softened. Add the beans, ketchup, vinegar, sugar, soy sauce, mustard, stock and paprika and simmer for another 15 minutes. Season with salt and pepper, then scatter the chopped coriander on top.

2 Preheat the oven to 200°C/180°C Fan/Gas 6. Place the tortillas on the work surface and divide the chicken mixture between them. Roll up the tortillas and place them in a greased ovenproof dish. Scatter the grated cheese on top and bake in the preheated oven for 15–20 minutes until golden. Serve with soured cream if you like.

A chain of piri-piri chicken restaurants has been taking over the high street in recent years and it seems like everyone is going crazy for this fiery dish. It got me thinking that if piri piri works so well on chicken wings it's got to be amazing in a burger, so I made some! I love serving these in crusty rolls with cooling, creamy home-made slaw. **SERVES 4**

PIRI-PIRI CHICKEN BURGERS

1 onion, roughly chopped
2 garlic cloves, peeled
2 red chillies
1 small piece of fresh
  root ginger, peeled
500g chicken thighs,
  skinless and boneless
60g fresh breadcrumbs
1 egg yolk
1/2 tsp smoked paprika
juice of 1 lime
olive oil
4 crusty rolls
sea salt
black pepper

*Red cabbage and
  mustard slaw*
1/4 red cabbage, shredded
1 small red onion,
  very finely sliced
1 carrot, grated
3 tbsp mayonnaise
1 tsp wholegrain mustard

1 Put the onion, garlic, chilli and ginger in a food processor and blitz to form a paste. Add the chicken thighs and pulse to break them down, but it's fine to leave a few slightly larger pieces of chicken in the mixture. Season with salt and pepper, then add the breadcrumbs, egg yolk, paprika and finally the lime juice. Mix thoroughly, then divide the mixture into 4 and shape into burgers. Cover them with cling film and leave to chill in the fridge for 30 minutes.

2 To make the slaw, put the cabbage, onion and carrot in a bowl. Add the mayonnaise and mustard, then season with salt and pepper. Mix thoroughly and leave for 15 minutes or so before serving to allow the flavours to develop.

3 Preheat the oven to 200°C/180°C Fan/Gas 6. Heat a little oil in an ovenproof pan and fry the burgers for 2–3 minutes on each side. Place them in the oven and cook for 10–12 minutes or until cooked through. Serve the burgers on the crusty rolls with the slaw on the side. These burgers are great cooked on a barbecue too!

My dad used to make a great chicken noodle soup for us when we were kids. We loved it – the noodles bulked out the soup and made it a highly satisfying meal for us all. I like to think my version has moved on from those days and the addition of miso, which is a fermented soya bean paste, gives a real depth of flavour. Miso is available in most supermarkets and in Asian grocery stores. SERVES 4

MISO CHICKEN NOODLE BROTH

olive oil
300g chicken mince
(or use 3–4 chicken
thighs – see p. 137)
1 thumb-sized piece
of fresh root ginger,
peeled and sliced
3 garlic cloves, sliced
1 small leek, shredded
1 litre chicken stock
1 tbsp miso paste
2 pak choi, quartered
150g beansprouts
1 tbsp soy sauce
250g soba noodles
2 tbsp chopped fresh
coriander
1 red chilli, finely sliced
1 lime, quartered
black pepper

1 Heat a dash of oil in a saucepan and fry the chicken mince for 5–6 minutes or until browned. Add the ginger, garlic and leek and cook gently for 3–4 minutes.

2 Pour in the chicken stock, bring to the boil, then simmer for 20 minutes. Add the miso paste, pak choi and beansprouts and cook for another 3 minutes. Season with soy sauce and pepper.

3 Meanwhile, cook the noodles in boiling water for 6–7 minutes, or according to the packet instructions, then drain.

4 Serve some noodles into each bowl and add spoonfuls of pak choi and beansprouts. Ladle over the chicken-rich soup and garnish with coriander and chilli. Serve with a wedge of lime to squeeze over the soup.

I love to serve this dish when we are lucky enough to get some good summer weather. You can prepare all of the elements ahead of time, then cook the koftas just before serving – they're great cooked on a barbecue too. Chermoula is a North African herb sauce and marinade, packed full of immense flavours. It's very versatile – I like to add a couple of spoonfuls to a Moroccan tagine or some grilled salmon. **SERVES 4**

CHERMOULA KOFTA SALAD

500g turkey mince
40g fresh breadcrumbs
2 x 400g cans of chickpeas, drained and rinsed
½ red chilli, deseeded and chopped
½ red onion, peeled and sliced
2 tbsp natural yoghurt
olive oil
2 handfuls of baby spinach, washed
sea salt
black pepper

Chermoula sauce
3 tbsp chopped coriander
2 tbsp chopped flat-leaf parsley
½ red onion, roughly chopped
1 garlic clove, peeled
1 tsp smoked paprika
½ tsp cumin
½ tsp chopped fresh coriander
40ml olive oil
juice of ½ lemon

1 First make the chermoula sauce. Blitz all the ingredients together in a mini blender or food processor to form a paste. Set this aside while you prepare the rest of the dish.

2 Put the mince in a large bowl and add the breadcrumbs and half the chermoula sauce. Season with salt and pepper, then shape the mixture into 8 sausage shapes. Place these on a tray, cover with cling film and chill in the fridge for 30 minutes.

3 Mix the chickpeas, chilli and red onion with the yoghurt, then stir in the rest of the chermoula sauce. Season with salt and pepper.

4 Heat a dash of olive oil in a non-stick pan and fry the koftas for 15–18 minutes, turning them until coloured on all sides and cooked through. Alternatively, cook them on a barbecue. To serve, spoon the chickpea salad on to a bed of baby spinach and top with the koftas.

My bro Wesley put me on to this dish after numerous trips to Thailand. Pad Thai is *the* essential street food of Bangkok. It has just the right balance of flavours and textures and it's a great sharing dish – everything you could ask for in a meal. There is a little bit of preparation to do, but once you start cooking it's go, go, go, and the food is on your plate in minutes. If you don't like the sound of turkey with prawns, leave out the shellfish, but promise me you will try it this way once. If you cannot find tamarind blocks, you can buy jars of prepared tamarind in the deli aisle at the supermarket. SERVES 4

BANGING TURKEY PAD THAI

300g flat rice noodles
olive oil
300g turkey mince
100g shelled raw prawns
2 eggs, beaten
100g beansprouts
4 spring onions, finely
   sliced

Pad Thai sauce
30g tamarind block
50ml just-boiled water
1 onion, roughly chopped
5 garlic cloves, peeled
vegetable oil
2 tbsp dark brown sugar
1 tbsp nam pla (fish sauce)
   or soy sauce

Garnish
20g salted peanuts, crushed
1 tbsp dried red chilli flakes
1 tbsp chopped fresh
   coriander
1 lime, cut into wedges,
   for serving

1 First make the pad Thai sauce. Put the tamarind block in the 50ml of water and leave to soak for 20 minutes, then pass it through a sieve and set aside. Put the onion and garlic in a food processor and blend to a purée. Heat a little vegetable oil in a saucepan and cook the onion purée over a medium heat for 5 minutes. Add the sugar, nam pla and tamarind liquor, then cook for another couple of minutes. Set aside.

2 Cook the noodles in boiling water until softened, according to the packet instructions, then drain and set aside.

3 Heat a dash of olive oil in a large wok-style pan and fry the turkey mince over a high heat for 10–12 minutes until cooked through. Fry the prawns for a minute or so until pink, then add the drained noodles, and continue cooking for a couple more minutes. Push the noodles to the side of the pan. Tip in the beaten eggs, cook for about 5 seconds, then stir them into the noodles.

4 Add the pad Thai sauce to the pan and cook for a couple of minutes. Add the beansprouts and spring onions, then garnish with peanuts, chilli flakes and coriander. Serve with wedges of lime.

I often serve this when family or friends are round for dinner. It's a fantastic sharing dish – everyone can help themselves, building their own plateful to their individual tastes. I like to eat my fajita with a dollop of soured cream and a grating of Cheddar cheese as well as my sides of spicy salsa and guacamole. **SERVES 4**

SMOKY TURKEY FAJITAS

olive oil
400g turkey mince
2 red peppers, cut into batons
1 green pepper, cut into batons
1 red onion, peeled and sliced
1 tsp smoked paprika
1 tsp ground cumin
1/2 tsp ground coriander
8 tortillas
soured cream, to serve
grated Cheddar cheese,
   to serve

My guacamole
2 ripe avocados
1/2 red onion, very finely diced
1/2 garlic clove, finely diced
1 red chilli, very finely diced
juice of 1 lime
2 tbsp chopped fresh
   coriander
sea salt
black pepper

Stunningly easy salsa
200g baby plum tomatoes
1/2 red onion, finely diced
1/2 red chilli, finely diced
2 tbsp chopped fresh coriander
juice of 1 lime
20ml olive oil

1 To make the guacamole, mash the avocado flesh, discarding the peel and stones. Add the diced onion, garlic and chilli, then mix in the lime juice and chopped coriander. Season with salt and pepper.

2 To make the salsa, put the tomatoes, onion, chilli and coriander in a blender and blitz for a few seconds. Tip the mixture into a bowl, season with salt and pepper, then dress with the lime juice and olive oil.

3 Heat a frying pan until really hot, add a dash of oil and fry the turkey mince until browned – about 7–8 minutes. Remove it from the pan and set aside. Add a little more oil to the pan and cook the peppers and onion for 3–4 minutes – they should still retain their crunch. Tip the turkey back into the pan and add the spices, then cook for another 1–2 minutes.

4 Warm the tortillas in the oven for a couple of minutes, then bring everything to the table and let everyone put their own fajitas together with some soured cream and cheese.

Turkey is one of the leanest meats on the market, so if you are looking to cut down the fat content of your meals without compromising on flavour, this is a recipe to try. It combines the aromatic flavours of Thailand with the great British barbecue so you can't go wrong! SERVES 4

THAI TURKEY BURGERS

2 shallots, peeled
2 garlic cloves, peeled
1 small piece of fresh root
   ginger, peeled
½ red chilli, deseeded
1 tbsp nam pla (fish sauce)
juice of 1 lime
500g turkey mince
1 tbsp red Thai curry paste
1 egg yolk
80g fresh breadcrumbs
2 tbsp chopped fresh
   coriander
olive oil
4 crusty rolls
watercress, for serving
sea salt
black pepper

1 Put the shallots, garlic, ginger, chilli, nam pla and lime juice in a blender and whizz to make a fine paste.

2 Put the mince in a bowl and add the paste you've just made, the red Thai curry paste, egg yolk, breadcrumbs and fresh coriander. Season with salt and pepper, then mix until thoroughly combined. Divide the mixture into 4 and shape into burgers, then cover them with cling film and chill in the fridge for 30 minutes to help set the shape.

3 Preheat the oven to 200°C/180°C Fan/Gas 6. Heat an ovenproof pan on the hob, add a little oil and cook the burgers for 2–3 minutes on each side. Transfer the pan to the preheated oven for 10–12 minutes or until the burgers are cooked through. Alternatively, cook them on a barbecue. Serve with crusty rolls and watercress.

Yoghurt has been scientifically proven to help meats take on more flavour during marinating – an essential part of any tandoori dish. When I go to my local curry house I always end up scoffing something from the tandoor, such as a mixed grill or some koftas. This is my take on a tandoori. It has bags of flavour and there's a cooling raita to serve alongside it. SERVES 2

TANDOORI TURKEY KOFTAS

1 tbsp garam masala
1 tsp ground coriander
1 tsp chilli powder
1 tsp paprika
1/2 tsp turmeric
60ml plain natural yoghurt
1 small piece of fresh root
   ginger, peeled and grated
2 garlic cloves, crushed
400g turkey mince
olive oil
sea salt
black pepper

Cumin-spiked raita
1/2 cucumber, peeled,
   deseeded and diced
100ml plain natural yoghurt
2 tbsp chopped fresh mint
1/2 tsp ground cumin
1 tsp sugar
sea salt
black pepper

1 Mix the spices in a bowl and add the yoghurt, ginger and garlic. Add the mince, season with salt and pepper, then shape the mixture into sausage-shaped koftas. Cover the koftas with cling film and leave them to marinate for at least an hour.

2 To make the raita, mix the cucumber, yoghurt, mint, cumin and sugar in a bowl and leave to stand for 10 minutes before serving. Season with salt and pepper.

3 Preheat the oven to 200°C/180°C Fan/Gas 6. Heat a dash of oil in a non-stick ovenproof pan and cook the koftas on the hob for 8 minutes until coloured on all sides. Transfer them to the preheated oven for 6–8 minutes or until cooked through. Leave to rest for 5 minutes, then thread them on to skewers and serve with the raita.

Did you know this very popular salad originated in Tijuana, Mexico? There are many variations, but one thing we all agree on in my household is definitely no anchovies. Always make sure you dress your salad leaves just before serving so that they stay nice and crisp. SERVES 4

TURKEY CAESAR SALAD

400g turkey mince
olive oil
100g smoked. cubed
    pancetta
2 slices of white bread,
    cubed
4 baby gem lettuces
1 avocado, peeled,
    stoned and sliced
Parmesan cheese,
    for shavings
sea salt
black pepper

Dressing
5 tbsp mayonnaise
50g Parmesan cheese,
    grated
juice of ½ lemon
½ clove garlic, crushed
1 tsp Dijon mustard

1 Place the mince into a large bowl and season with a good pinch of salt and pepper. Divide the mixture into golf ball-sized meatballs, cover with cling film and leave them to chill in the fridge for 20 minutes if you have time. Heat a dash of oil in a non-stick frying pan and cook the meatballs for 12–14 minutes until coloured all over and cooked through.

2 Place the pancetta in a frying pan with a dash of olive oil and cook until crispy. Remove the pancetta from the pan and place it on some kitchen paper to drain. Add the cubes of bread to the pan and cook until golden, then remove and leave them to drain on some kitchen paper.

3 To make the dressing, whisk together the mayonnaise, Parmesan, lemon juice, garlic and mustard in a small jug, then season. Separate the lettuce leaves and toss them with the dressing.

4 To serve, divide the lettuce between the bowls, top with some crispy pancetta, slices of avocado, fried bread croutons and finally the meatballs. Shave some Parmesan on to the salad and serve right away.

My version of one of Britain's best-loved dishes has everything you could want from a curry – it's creamy, full of flavour and has a hint of chilli. Ready-made tikka masala pastes are readily available, but it's the addition of the ginger and other spices that takes this recipe to a new level – and there's not a drop of red food colouring in sight. For a lower-fat version use half-fat coconut milk. Serve with some pilau rice (see p. 199) and naan bread. SERVES 4

TURKEY TIKKA MASALA

2 onions, peeled
3 garlic cloves, peeled
1 thumb-sized piece of
    fresh root ginger, peeled
1 red chilli
450g turkey mince
2 tbsp tikka masala paste
olive oil
1/2 tsp turmeric
1 stick of cinnamon
400g passata
1 x 400ml can of coconut milk
40g ground almonds
1 tsp sugar
1 tbsp chopped fresh
    coriander, to garnish
sea salt
black pepper

1 Place 1 of the onions in a blender with the garlic, ginger and chilli and blitz until smooth. Spoon half of this purée into a bowl and add the turkey mince and 1 tablespoon of the tikka masala paste. Season with salt and pepper and mix well. Shape into golf ball-sized meatballs. Heat a little oil in a non-stick pan and fry the turkey balls until slightly browned, then set aside.

2 Slice the other onion and add it to the pan with a dash more oil and the rest of the purée. Fry for 4–5 minutes, then add the turmeric, cinnamon and remaining tablespoon of tikka paste and fry for another minute.

3 Add the passata, coconut milk and ground almonds and bring everything to a simmer, then place the turkey balls back into the pan. Cover the pan with a lid and simmer the curry for 20–25 minutes or until the turkey is cooked through. Add the sugar, then stir in the fresh coriander just before serving.

Who doesn't like a good lasagne? It's an Italian dish we've really taken to our hearts. As a change from the classic beef, I've come up with a spicy version using turkey mince. Simply served with a crisp side salad, this makes a great family supper. **SERVES 4**

TURKEY CHILLI LASAGNE

olive oil
400g turkey mince
1 large onion, very finely diced
1 green pepper, diced
1 green chilli, diced
4 garlic cloves, crushed
1 tbsp chopped fresh
  thyme (leaves picked
  from the stems)
150ml red wine
½ tsp smoked paprika
1 tsp cumin
1 x 400g can of red kidney
  beans
2 x 400g cans of chopped
  tomatoes
1 tsp sugar
fresh lasagne
  (about 9 sheets)
70g Cheddar cheese,
  grated
sea salt
black pepper

White sauce
50g unsalted butter
50g plain flour
500ml milk

1 Heat a non-stick frying pan, add a dash of oil and brown the mince for 5–6 minutes. Remove the mince from the pan and set it aside.

2 Using the same pan, add a little more oil and cook the onion, pepper, chilli, garlic and thyme for 5 minutes until softened. Pour in the wine and continue cooking until the liquid is reduced by half. Put the mince back in the pan with the paprika, cumin, beans and tomatoes. Reduce the heat to a simmer and cook for 10 minutes. Add the sugar and season with salt and pepper.

3 To make the white sauce, melt the butter in a small pan over a medium heat. Whisk in the flour and cook for 2 minutes while stirring, then pour in the milk and continue whisking until it comes to a boil. Reduce the heat and simmer the sauce for 5 minutes, stirring occasionally. Season with salt and pepper. Preheat the oven to 200°C/180°C Fan/Gas 6.

4 Grease an ovenproof dish, measuring about 33 x 23cm, with a little oil. To assemble the lasagne, start with a layer of white sauce, then alternate layers of lasagne, turkey mixture and sauce, finishing with white sauce. Sprinkle grated cheese on top and cook in the preheated oven for 40 minutes until piping hot and golden.

I love this hot and sour soup, which always tastes so light and fresh. It's perfect for the hot summer evenings, but the warmth of the ginger and chilli makes it good for a crisp winter's night too. You'll find all these ingredients in your supermarket so give it a try. I promise you won't be disappointed. **SERVES 4**

TURKEY TOM YUM SOUP

400g turkey mince
1 egg yolk
2 tbsp chopped fresh
   coriander
vegetable oil
1 thumb-sized piece of
   fresh root ginger, peeled
1–2 red chillies, deseeded,
   plus extra for garnish
   (optional)
4 garlic cloves, peeled
1 onion, roughly diced
1 tbsp nam pla (fish sauce)
1 lemon grass stalk
1 litre chicken stock
2 tbsp brown sugar
150g oyster mushrooms,
   wiped and sliced
juice of 1–2 limes
fresh mint, for serving
6 spring onions, finely sliced
sea salt
black pepper

1 Put the mince in a bowl and mix it with the egg yolk and chopped coriander, then season with salt and pepper. Shape the mixture into golf ball-sized meatballs, then cover with cling film and chill them in the fridge for 20 minutes if you have time. Heat a dash of oil in a non-stick saucepan and fry the meatballs over a medium heat for 7–8 minutes until browned all over. Remove them from the pan and set aside.

2 Place the ginger, chilli (1 or 2 depending on how much heat you like), garlic, onion and nam pla in a small blender and blitz to a fine paste. Bash the lemon grass with a rolling pin to release the flavoursome oils. Add a little oil to the pan you used for the meatballs and fry the paste and lemon grass for 3–4 minutes over a medium heat. Add the stock and bring it to the boil, then put the meatballs back in the pan and add the sugar. Turn the heat down and simmer the soup for about 15 minutes.

3 Add the mushrooms and cook for a further 2–3 minutes, then squeeze in the lime juice to taste. Ladle the soup into bowls and garnish with fresh mint and sliced spring onions – and some extra chilli if you like it hot!

Spring rolls can be stodgy and greasy, but not these! The flavour comes from the spicy mince and you get a fresh-tasting crunch from the vegetables. You'll find spring-roll wrappers in Chinese supermarkets and they freeze very well so stock up. The spring rolls are deep fried so be very careful as you do this and never leave hot oil unattended. Serve with a dipping sauce (see p. 202). MAKES 8

THAI TURKEY SPRING ROLLS

olive oil
300g turkey mince
2 garlic cloves, crushed
1 tbsp red Thai curry paste
150g Savoy cabbage,
    shredded
1 tbsp sweet chilli sauce
juice of 1/2 lime
3 tbsp chopped fresh
    coriander
16 large spring-roll wrappers
100g beansprouts
1 small carrot,
    cut into thin strips
3 spring onions,
    cut into thin strips
30g salted peanuts, chopped
1 tsp cornflour
1 tsp water
vegetable oil, for deep frying

1 Heat a dash of oil in a non-stick frying pan and fry the mince for 5–6 minutes. Add the garlic, curry paste and cabbage and cook for a couple more minutes. Stir in the sweet chilli and lime juice, then cool before adding the coriander.

2 Take 2 spring-roll wrappers and put them 1 on top of the other for extra strength. Place them on a work surface in a diamond shape, with the points facing an imaginary north, south, east and west. Take a portion of the turkey and cabbage mixture and shape it into a sausage shape, then place it on the bottom third of the diamond, closest to you. Top with some beansprouts, carrot, spring onion and peanuts. Fold the corners in and roll up the wrapper from the bottom until the filling is fully enclosed. Mix the cornflour and water to make a paste and use it to seal the pastry as you make the last fold. Repeat with the rest of the wrappers and filling.

3 Fill a large pan about a third full with vegetable oil and heat to 180°C. If you don't have a cooking thermometer, test the temperature with a piece of bread – if it turns golden in a minute, the oil is hot enough. Carefully add the spring rolls, a few at a time, and fry them for 2–3 minutes. Remove and drain on kitchen paper before serving.

If you are cooking for just the two of you at Christmas and don't want the hassle of cooking a huge turkey, this is the recipe you need. It looks like you've made a massive effort but it's easy to do and you can prepare everything ahead of time in individual portions, then sit down for a well-deserved sherry. Serve with the classic trimmings – roast potatoes (see p. 196), Brussels sprouts and beautiful gravy (see p. 202). And don't forget the pigs in blankets. **SERVES 2**

STUFFED TURKEY ESCALOPES

2 turkey breast escalopes
olive oil
200g turkey mince
1 egg white
½ onion, very finely chopped
50g shelled pistachios
50g dried apricots, chopped
1 tsp finely chopped sage
6 slices of Parma ham
sea salt
black pepper

1 Place an escalope between 2 sheets of cling film and bash it with a rolling pin to flatten it. Be careful not to beat right through and split the meat. Bash the other escalope in the same way.

2 Heat a little oil in a frying pan, add the turkey mince and cook for 5 minutes, being careful not to let it colour. Tip it into a bowl and leave to cool.

3 Mix the egg white into the cooled turkey mince, then add the onion, pistachios, apricots and sage. Season with salt and pepper.

4 Lay 3 slices of Parma ham side by side on a sheet of cling film. Place an escalope on top, then add half of the stuffing. Using the cling film, roll up the escalope tightly, with the ham around it, and twist the ends. Do the same with the second escalope, then chill them in the fridge until you are ready to cook.

5 Preheat the oven to 220°C/200°C Fan/Gas 6. Put the escalopes in a roasting tin, remove the cling film and cook for 20 minutes. Turn the oven down to 180°C/160°C Fan/Gas 4 and roast for another 40 minutes until cooked through. Use a skewer to check that the juices run clear. Remove from the oven, cover with foil and leave to rest for at least 10 minutes before slicing and serving.

The koftas are just right with this salad which contains quinoa, which is an amazing superfood. Quinoa is very high in protein and I like to cook it in the same way as couscous or rice. Jazz it up with loads of fresh herbs and it's healthy and delicious. You'll need about 12 bamboo skewers for this recipe. SERVES 4

LEAN TURKEY KOFTAS WITH QUINOA AND POMEGRANATE SALAD

500g lean turkey breast
   mince
3 garlic cloves, crushed
1 tsp ground cumin
grated zest of 1/2 lemon
2 tbsp chopped flat-leaf
   parsley
sea salt
black pepper

*Quinoa and pomegranate
   salad*
200g quinoa
30g walnuts, toasted
seeds from 1/2 pomegranate
100g baby plum tomatoes,
   halved
2 tbsp chopped flat-leaf
   parsley
2 tbsp chopped fresh mint
juice of 1/2 lemon
extra virgin olive oil,
   to dress

1 Soak the skewers in cold water for about 10 minutes so they don't burn too much.

2 Put the turkey mince in a bowl and add the garlic, cumin, lemon zest and parsley. Mix well, then season with salt and pepper. Shape some of the mixture around each skewer in a rough, slightly flattened oval shape. You should have about 12. Chill in the fridge for 20 minutes,

3 Cook the quinoa in a pan of salted boiling water for 10–12 minutes, or according to the packet instructions. The husks come away easily when the grains are done. Toast the walnuts in a dry pan for a couple of minutes, tossing them regularly and watching that they don't burn. To remove the jewel-like seeds from the pomegranate, cut the pomegranate in half around its middle. Place it in a large bowl of water and separate out the seeds. That way you don't get pomegranate juice all over your clothes! Add the pomegranate seeds to the quinoa with the rest of the ingredients, then dress with olive oil and lemon juice to taste. Season with salt and pepper.

4 Cook the koftas on a preheated griddle pan over a medium heat for 12–14 minutes, then serve with the salad.

CHAPTER 5

FISH MINCE

You won't find minced fish in your local fishmonger or supermarket, but don't let that stop you making some amazing dishes. Salmon, prawns and other types of seafood can be minced or blitzed in a food processor very successfully to make recipes such as fishcakes or even fish burgers. Here are a few of my favourites, including cod and crab bonbons (see p. 174) and fragrant lemon grass salmon skewers (see p. 177).

I have fond childhood memories of trips to the local chippy, where you had a choice of battered fish, sausages, saveloys or potato-heavy fishcakes served with a limp tartare sauce. I still have a place in my heart for fishcakes and once I dip into that tangy tartare sauce there's no stopping me. I use the flesh from baked potatoes for making my fishcakes, as I find it gives a lighter texture than mash. SERVES 4

CLASSIC FISHCAKES WITH TARTARE SAUCE

300g Maris Piper potatoes
olive oil
300g cod or similar white fish, skinned
3 spring onions, sliced
2 tbsp chopped flat-leaf parsley
50g plain flour
50g dry breadcrumbs
2 eggs, beaten
sea salt
black pepper

Tartare sauce
5 tbsp mayonnaise
1 tsp Dijon mustard
3 cornichons, finely chopped
1 tbsp chopped flat-leaf parsley
squeeze of lemon juice, to taste

1 Bake the potatoes at 190°C/170°C Fan/Gas 5, for about an hour or until softened, or in a microwave for 15 minutes. Cut the potatoes in half, scoop out the flesh and fork it through to give a light and fluffy texture. Set aside.

2 Mix all the tartare sauce ingredients in a bowl, cover and put it in the fridge until needed.

3 Heat a non-stick frying pan, add a dash of oil and fry the cod for 4–5 minutes. Set it aside to cool slightly, then mash it with the back of a fork. In a bowl, mix the potatoes with the spring onions and parsley, then season with salt and pepper. Add the fish and stir it through gently. Divide the mixture into 8 and shape it into cakes.

4 Spread the flour and breadcrumbs on separate plates and season the flour. Beat the eggs in a bowl. Dust each fishcake in flour, dip it in the beaten egg and then the breadcrumbs to coat. Heat some more oil in the frying pan and fry the fishcakes for 2–3 minutes on each side until browned. Serve with the tartare sauce.

These flavour-packed little beauties make a perfect starter or canapé. The combination of cod and crab is a marriage made in heaven, but any flaky white fish, such as pollack, whiting or coley, will do. Serve with a nice sharp dipping sauce (see p. 202) or some mayo flavoured with lime juice (see p. 203). SERVES 4

COD AND CRAB BONBONS

olive oil
300g cod fillets, skinned
1 tbsp grated fresh root ginger
1 large shallot, diced
1 tsp Thai red curry paste
170g canned crab meat
   chunks, drained
2 tbsp double cream
2 tbsp chopped fresh
   coriander
1 red chilli, deseeded
   and diced
juice of 1 lime
40g plain flour
80g dry breadcrumbs
2 eggs
vegetable oil, for deep frying
sea salt
black pepper

1 Heat a non-stick pan on the hob, add a splash of oil and cook the cod for 3–4 minutes. Transfer the fish to a plate and mince it with a fork, then set it aside to cool slightly.

2 Using the same pan, cook the grated ginger and shallot for 2–3 minutes, then add the Thai paste and cook for a further minute. Tip this into a bowl and add the crab, cream, coriander, chilli and lime juice, then season with salt and pepper. Finally, add the cod and gently fold it through the mixture. Roll the mixture into golf ball-sized pieces, cover with cling film and chill them in the fridge for 20 minutes.

3 Spread the flour and breadcrumbs on separate plates and season the flour. Beat the eggs in a bowl. Roll the balls in the seasoned flour, dip them in the egg, then coat with breadcrumbs.

4 Pour the oil into a large pan and heat to 185°C. Always be very careful when heating oil and never leave hot oil unattended. If you don't have a cooking thermometer, drop a small piece of bread into the oil and if it turns golden brown in a minute, the oil is hot enough. Deep fry the bonbons, a few at a time, for 1–2 minutes or until golden brown, then remove and drain them on kitchen paper.

Lemon grass imparts a beautiful citrus flavour to many Asian-inspired dishes and we're getting used to seeing it on supermarket shelves. I simply bash the stalks with a rolling pin or finely chop them to use in delights such as Thai green curry or a spicy rendang. You can also find lemon grass in a pre-prepared form, normally in a tube, and I find the texture of this is better than fresh for this recipe. For ease, I thread the fish koftas on to skewers after cooking or, for an added twist, you could serve them on sticks of lemon grass instead of skewers. Serve with the dipping sauce. SERVES 4

LEMON GRASS SALMON SKEWERS

300g salmon fillets, skinned
1 large shallot, chopped
1 egg yolk
1 tbsp lemon grass paste
1 tbsp grated fresh root ginger
1 tbsp fresh breadcrumbs
1 tsp sesame seeds, toasted
olive oil
1 tbsp chopped fresh
    coriander, for garnish
sea salt
black pepper

Dipping sauce
1 tbsp sugar
1 tbsp water
3 tbsp soy sauce
juice of 1 lime
1/2 red chilli, finely diced
1 tbsp finely chopped
    fresh coriander

1 Place the salmon fillets in a blender or food processor and pulse for a few seconds. Don't over process – you want to break the fish down but you don't want to make it into a paste. Tip the fish into a bowl, then add the shallot, egg yolk, lemon grass paste, ginger and breadcrumbs. Leave the mixture to marinate for at least 20 minutes, if possible, then season well.

2 Divide the mixture into 8, then shape into oval-shaped koftas. Cover them with cling film and leave to chill in the fridge for 30 minutes to help them keep their shape. Toast the sesame seeds in a dry pan for a minute or so, shaking the pan often and watching that the seeds don't burn.

3 Heat a non-stick pan, add a dash of oil and cook the fish koftas for 2 minutes on each side, then thread them on to skewers. Before serving, sprinkle the koftas with toasted sesame seeds and garnish with fresh coriander.

4 To make the dipping sauce, dissolve the sugar in the water, then add the rest of the ingredients. Add extra lime juice if you like.

Wasabi is a Japanese horseradish paste, used as a condiment for sushi. Vibrant green in colour, it's really fiery and I love it. If you can't get wasabi, use a teaspoon of creamed horseradish instead. Japanese panko breadcrumbs are stocked in many supermarkets and their crisp texture makes for a lighter coating than ordinary breadcrumbs. SERVES 4

SALMON BURGERS WITH WASABI MAYO

200g Maris Piper potatoes, cubed
olive oil
300g salmon fillet, skinned
2 tbsp chopped fresh coriander, plus extra for garnish
grated zest of 1/2 lime
1/2 onion, very finely chopped
2 eggs
40g plain flour
60g panko breadcrumbs
4 burger buns
rocket, for serving
sea salt
black pepper

Wasabi mayo
100ml mayonnaise
1/2 tsp wasabi
juice of 1/2 lime
2 spring onions, sliced

1 Put the potatoes in a large pan of salted water, bring to the boil and cook for 8–10 minutes, or until tender. Drain, then leave them for 5 minutes to dry off and cool.

2 Add a dash of oil to a non-stick frying pan and cook the salmon over a medium to high heat for 3–4 minutes or until cooked three-quarters of the way through. Turn the fish over, then switch off the heat and leave it in the pan to finish cooking for 2–3 minutes before transferring it to a plate.

3 Tip the potatoes into a bowl and break them down roughly with a fork. Mix them with the 2 tablespoons of coriander, lime zest, onion and 1 beaten egg, then season. Flake the fish and gently fold it into the mixture. Divide this into 4, then shape into burgers, cover with cling film and chill for 20 minutes.

4 To make the wasabi mayo, mix the ingredients in a bowl, then set aside.

5 Spread the flour and breadcrumbs on plates and beat the remaining egg in a bowl. Season the flour. Dust the burgers with flour, then dip them into the egg and then the breadcrumbs to coat. Add a splash more oil to the pan and cook the burgers for 2–3 minutes on each side. Toast the buns, then serve the burgers in the buns with rocket, coriander and dollops of wasabi mayo.

CHAPTER 6
DESSERTS

It's OK – the puds in this chapter don't contain mince, but I do have a very sweet tooth so I just had to throw in some of my favourites. The recipes are 100 per cent meat-free and all very delicious I can promise you.

Of course, mince pies, the traditional Christmas treat, used to contain minced meat. We've moved on from this now, but I've included my mince pie samosas (see p. 191) as a tongue-in-cheek tribute to this old recipe. Hope you enjoy them!

Once upon a time, I was one of a long list of *Masterchef* contestants who tried, and failed, to serve up a perfect chocolate fondant. Unfortunately for me, I presented my cakey fondant to none other than Stephen Fry. I'll leave you to imagine what he said about it! I promised myself that would never happen again, so I've come up with a foolproof recipe. Follow this and you will succeed every single time. SERVES 4

CHEAT'S CHOCOLATE FONDANT

180g unsalted butter,
   plus extra for greasing
180g dark chocolate
   (70% cocoa)
3 medium eggs
3 medium egg yolks
90g caster sugar
40g plain flour
1/2 tsp baking powder
10g cocoa powder
small pinch of salt
unsalted butter, for greasing
4 dark chocolate truffles
vanilla ice cream,
   for serving

1 Place a heatproof bowl over a pan of gently simmering water, making sure the bottom of the bowl does not touch the water. Add the butter and chocolate and allow them to melt. Carefully remove the bowl from the pan and set aside to cool slightly.

2 Preheat the oven to 210°C/190°C Fan/Gas 6½. Whisk the whole eggs, egg yolks and sugar together in a bowl until pale and fluffy. Sift the flour, baking powder and cocoa into the bowl, add a pinch of salt and fold them into the chocolate and butter mixture.

3 Butter 4 ramekin dishes or individual pudding basins. Fill each dish half-full with the chocolate mixture. Place a truffle in each, then top up with the rest of the chocolate mixture.

4 Place the ramekins on a baking tray and cook in the preheated oven for 12 minutes. Leave to stand for 1 minute, then turn the fondants out on to serving plates. Serve at once with some vanilla ice cream for the ultimate treat.

My Uncle Ed introduced me to this pudding. I know it sounds cheesy, but when I was a kid I truly thought it was the best thing I'd eaten in my life or would ever eat. Very easy and quick to make, this recipe is an Edwards' family tradition. Serve with some vanilla ice cream. **SERVES 6**

CHOCOLATE SURPRISE PUDDING

115g unsalted butter, softened, plus extra for greasing
115g caster sugar
2 eggs, beaten
1 tsp vanilla extract
85g self-raising flour, sifted
30g cocoa powder
pinch of salt
30ml milk

Sauce
120g soft brown sugar
30g cocoa powder
300ml boiling water

1 Preheat the oven to 180°C/160°C Fan/Gas 4 Grease a 33 x 23cm baking dish generously with butter.

2 Cream the butter and sugar together in a large bowl until light and fluffy. Beat in the eggs, a little at a time, and add the vanilla extract. Fold in the sifted flour and the cocoa and salt until combined, then add the milk – the mixture should have a medium-soft consistency. Spoon it into the baking dish.

3 Mix all the ingredients for the sauce in a bowl and stir well, then carefully pour it over the sponge mixture. Bake the pudding in the preheated oven for 40–45 minutes.

The combo of bananas, rum and raisins always brings a smile to my face. Top that off with a generous helping of butter-rich puff pastry and I'm in heaven. Tarte tatin can be made with apples and pears but trust me, banana is the way to go. Serve with ice cream that has been crusted with nuts for the ultimate indulgent touch. **SERVES 4**

TOFFEE BANANA TARTE TATIN

70g demerara sugar
70g unsalted butter
4 small under-ripe bananas, peeled and cut in half lengthways
40g juicy plump raisins
20ml rum
about 300g puff pastry
flour, for rolling
chocolate ice cream
20g pistachio nuts, crushed

1 Put an ovenproof frying pan, about 30cm in diameter, on the hob and add the sugar and butter. Let the butter melt and keep shaking the pan until the sugar has dissolved and the mixture has turned a dark caramel colour. Add the bananas and raisins, then continue cooking for 2–3 minutes. Add the rum and warm for 5–10 seconds before lighting it with a lighter to flambé the bananas briefly. Watch out for your eyebrows! Preheat the oven to 200°C/180°C Fan/Gas 6.

2 Roll out the puff pastry on a floured surface until is about 5mm thick. Cut out a disc of pastry that is slightly bigger than your pan. Carefully place the pastry over the bananas and try to tuck it under them where you can. Prick a hole in the top of the pastry.

3 Place the pan in the preheated oven and bake for 30–35 minutes. Remove the pan and let it stand for a minute, before carefully turning the tarte out upside down on to a plate – be careful, as the pan will be hot.

4 Using a scoop, make balls of ice cream and pop them in the freezer until needed. When you're ready, spread the crushed pistachios on a plate, roll the ice cream balls in them to coat and serve with the tart.

If you're nervous about making pastry you're not alone and you'll be pleased to hear that this recipe is fine made with bought shortcrust. The light fluffy frangipane screams of almonds and is enhanced by a generous dash of Amaretto, my favourite liqueur. Try to use cherries when they are in season, as they taste so much better. At other times, you could make this tart with apples, pears, plums or peaches. Serve with clotted cream or vanilla ice cream. SERVES 6

CHERRY FRANGIPANE TART

125g unsalted butter, softened
125g caster sugar
2 eggs
125g ground almonds
20g plain flour, plus extra for rolling
3 tbsp Amaretto liqueur
500g shortcrust pastry
3 tsp cherry jam
250g cherries, pitted and halved

1 To make the frangipane filling, put the butter and caster sugar in a bowl and cream until the mixture is light and fluffy – it's easiest to do this with an electric hand whisk. Add the eggs, 1 at a time, beating after each addition. Sift in the almonds and flour, then fold them into the butter and sugar until fully incorporated. Stir in the Amaretto, then leave in the fridge until needed.

2 Preheat the oven to 180°C/160°C Fan/Gas 4. Roll out the pastry on a floured surface until it is about 5mm thick and use it to line a 23cm loose-bottomed tart tin. Leave any excess pastry hanging over the edges. Prick the base with a fork, cover with foil and pour in some dried beans to keep the pastry flat. Bake the pastry case in the preheated oven for 15 minutes. Remove the foil and beans, then return the pastry to the oven for 5 minutes to crisp. Allow it to cool slightly and then carefully trim away any excess pastry with a knife. Leave the oven on.

3 Warm the jam in a small pan. Using a pastry brush, paint the jam on to the pastry base. Spread the frangipane mixture over the jam, then top with the halved cherries. Put the tart back in the oven and cook for 25–30 minutes. Serve hot or cold – delicious either way.

I couldn't write a cookbook based on mince without including my quick and easy version of the Christmas classic – mince pies. Traditionally, mince pies did actually contain meat, but now it's the sweet version that we all know and love. This quick and easy recipe is great if you have guests dropping in unexpectedly over the festive period. Serve with some vanilla custard or some double cream and dip away. Ho, ho, ho! MAKES ABOUT 16

MINCE PIE SAMOSAS

1 x 400g jar of good-quality
    mincemeat
50g chopped nuts
    (I love macadamias)
40ml brandy (optional)
1 pack of filo pastry
50g unsalted butter, melted,
    plus extra for greasing
icing sugar, for dusting

1 Tip the mincemeat into a bowl and stir in the nuts. If you are using brandy, stir that in too. Preheat the oven to 180°C/160°C Fan/Gas 4.

2 Take a sheet of filo, brush it with melted butter, then fold it over to make a long rectangle. Brush this with more butter and place a large spoonful of the mincemeat on the bottom left-hand corner of the pastry. Fold the corner over and continue folding corner to corner until the mixture is fully enclosed and you've used the whole strip of filo. Make the rest of the samosas in the same way until you've used up all your filling.

3 Place the samosas on a greased baking tray and bake them in the preheated oven for 20–25 minutes or until golden brown. Leave the samosas to cool for 10 minutes, then dust them with icing sugar before serving.

We are now officially a nation of brownie lovers and they seem to be popping up everywhere. You can buy very good ones, but they are expensive and nothing can beat eating them fresh out of the oven. I believe that a brownie should have a wafer-thin, papery skin on top and be moist and sticky on the inside. It's hard to check whether these cakes are cooked, as the normal test with a skewer won't work, so trust your instinct and follow these guidelines. MAKES 16

CHOCOLATE AND SOUR CHERRY BROWNIES

75g dried sour cherries
30ml Amaretto liqueur
250g unsalted butter,
    plus extra for greasing
250g dark chocolate
    (70% cocoa)
4 medium eggs
330g golden caster sugar
150g plain flour
1 tbsp cocoa powder
pinch of salt
100g macadamia nuts,
    chopped

1 Soak the cherries in the Amaretto for at least half an hour, then set to one side. Grease a 30 x 20cm baking tray with butter and line it with non-stick baking parchment.

2 Place a heatproof bowl over a pan of gently simmering water, making sure the bottom of the bowl is not touching the water. Add the butter and chocolate and allow them to melt. Carefully remove the bowl from the pan and set aside. Preheat the oven to 180°C/160°C Fan/Gas 4.

3 Meanwhile, beat the eggs and sugar in a bowl until light and fluffy – this will take about 5 minutes. Add the melted chocolate and butter and stir until fully combined. Sift in the flour, cocoa powder and salt, then fold them through the mixture gently. Add the nuts, cherries and any Amaretto that hasn't been soaked up.

4 Spoon the mixture into the greased and lined baking tray and bake in the preheated oven for about 30 minutes. Check that the brownies have a thin papery crust on top and a slightly gooey centre, then remove them from the oven and leave them to cool – if you can bear the wait!

CHAPTER 7

SIDE DISHES

BUTTERY MASH SERVES 4

800g Maris Piper potatoes
30g unsalted butter
about 60ml whole milk,
  warmed
sea salt
black pepper

1 Peel the potatoes and cut them into even-sized pieces. Put them in a saucepan of salted water, bring to the boil and cook until tender. Drain and leave them in a colander to cool briefly – this way the potatoes are not too wet when you start to mash them.

2 Tip the potatoes back into the pan and mash them, or pass them through a ricer, then stir in the butter until it has melted. Add the warm milk and season generously with salt and pepper.

PARSNIP MASH SERVES 4

400g parsnips
400g Maris Piper potatoes
30g unsalted butter
about 60ml whole milk,
  warmed
2 tbsp horseradish sauce
sea salt
black pepper

1 Peel the parsnips and potatoes and cut them into even-sized pieces. Put them in a pan of salted water, bring to the boil and cook until tender. Drain and leave them in a colander to cool briefly – this way the veg are not too wet when you start to mash.

2 Tip the parsnips and potatoes back into the pan and mash them, or pass them through a ricer, then stir in the butter until it has melted. Add the warm milk, then the horseradish sauce. Season generously with salt and pepper.

AMAZING ROAST POTATOES SERVES 4

1kg Maris Piper potatoes
60ml olive oil
1 garlic bulb, broken into
   cloves but not peeled
3–4 sprigs of fresh thyme
   or rosemary
sea salt
black pepper

1 Cut the potatoes into chunks and place them in a large saucepan of salted water. Bring to the boil and cook for 4–5 minutes, then drain. Leave the potatoes in a colander for 5 minutes to steam, then give them a quick toss to roughen up the edges.

2 Meanwhile, preheat the oven to 210°C/190°C Fan/Gas 6½. Pour the oil into a baking tray and put it in the oven to heat up. When the oil is hot, add the potatoes, quickly turning them to make sure they all have a good coating of oil. Scatter in the garlic cloves and herbs, then season with salt and pepper. Put the tray back into the oven and roast for about 1 hour. Turn the potatoes once or twice during this time to make sure they are crispy and golden all over. Serve at once.

SAUTÉ POTATOES SERVES 4

800g new potatoes
40g unsalted butter
small glug of olive oil
1 tbsp chopped fresh
   rosemary
1 garlic clove
sea salt
black pepper

1 Put the potatoes in a large saucepan of salted water, bring to the boil and cook for 7–8 minutes. Drain, then cut the potatoes in half lengthways.

2 Heat the butter and oil in a non-stick frying pan and sauté the potatoes until golden brown. Add the chopped rosemary and garlic, then cook for another minute. Season with salt and pepper, then serve immediately.

HERBY COUSCOUS SERVES 4

500ml chicken stock
250g couscous
50g flaked almonds
small bunch of flat-leaf
  parsley, chopped
small bunch of fresh
  coriander, chopped
juice of 1 lemon
30ml extra virgin olive oil
sea salt
black pepper

1 Heat the chicken stock in a pan. Put the couscous in a bowl and pour over the boiling stock, then cover with cling film and leave to stand for 5 minutes.

2 Put the almonds in a dry frying pan and cook briefly over a medium heat until toasted. Keep a careful eye on them, as they burn easily.

3 Fork through the couscous to separate the grains, then add the chopped herbs, toasted almonds, lemon juice and olive oil. Season with salt and pepper and gently mix everything together before serving.

FRUITY COUSCOUS SERVES 4

500ml vegetable stock
250g couscous
50g pine nuts
small bunch of fresh mint,
  chopped
50g dried apricots, chopped
juice of 1 lemon
30ml extra virgin olive oil
seeds from ½ pomegranate
  (see p. 62 for how
  to remove them)
sea salt
black pepper

1 Heat the vegetable stock in a pan. Put the couscous in a bowl and pour over the boiling stock, then cover with cling film and leave to stand for 5 minutes.

2 Put the pine nuts in a dry frying pan and cook briefly over a medium heat until toasted. Keep a careful eye on them, as they burn easily.

3 Fork through the couscous to separate the grains, then stir in the toasted pine nuts, chopped mint, apricots, lemon juice and olive oil. Season well with salt and pepper, then scatter the pomegranate seeds on top before serving.

MUSHROOM PILAF SERVES 4

olive oil
100g mushrooms,
  wiped and sliced
1 onion, sliced
2 garlic cloves, crushed
½ tsp turmeric
2 cardamom pods, crushed
250g brown basmati rice
500ml water
sea salt
black pepper

1 Heat a non-stick saucepan, add a splash of oil and fry the mushrooms until golden. Add the onion, garlic, turmeric and cardamom, then continue to cook for 5 minutes.

2 Add the rice to the pan and stir to give it a coating of oil, then pour in the water. Bring to the boil, then reduce the heat, cover the pan and cook over a low heat for 30–35 minutes or until the rice is tender. Season with salt and pepper. Remove the cardamom pods before serving.

JASMINE RICE SERVES 4

250g jasmine rice
500ml just-boiled water
sea salt

1 Tip the rice into a non-stick saucepan. Pour in the just-boiled water and place the pan over a medium heat. Add a good pinch of salt, stir, then cover the pan and turn the heat down as low as you can.

2 Cook for 15–20 minutes until the rice is tender and all the water has been absorbed. Fluff up the rice with a fork before serving.

COURGETTE
RIBBON SALAD SERVES 2

2 courgettes
½ red onion, thinly sliced
5 radishes, trimmed and
   thinly sliced
½ red chilli, deseeded
   and finely diced

Vinaigrette
1 tbsp sherry vinegar
3 tbsp olive oil
1 tsp honey
½ tsp Dijon mustard
½ garlic clove, crushed
sea salt
black pepper

1 Using a vegetable peeler, slice the courgettes into thin ribbons. Put them in a serving bowl with the sliced onion and radishes.

2 Whisk together the vinaigrette ingredients, then season with salt and pepper. Add the dressing to the salad with the chilli, toss and then serve.

FETA AND BEETROOT SALAD WITH POMEGRANATE DRESSING SERVES 2

50ml pomegranate juice
extra virgin olive oil
200g new potatoes
20g unsalted butter
200g cooked beetroot
150g feta cheese, crumbled
2 handfuls of pea shoots
sea salt
black pepper

1 Pour the pomegranate juice into a small pan and place over a medium heat. Cook until the juice is reduced and syrupy. Remove the pan from the heat and set aside to cool, then add the olive oil and season with salt and pepper.

2 Put the potatoes in a pan of salted water and bring to the boil. Cook until they're almost done, then drain and cut in half lengthways. Heat a frying pan and add the butter, then sauté the potatoes until golden brown. Season to taste.

3 Slice the cooked beetroot and place the slices on a serving plate. Crumble the feta cheese on top, then add the pea shoots and sautéed potatoes. Drizzle over the pomegranate dressing and serve.

GRAVY SERVES 4

1 onion, quartered
1 carrot, cut into 4 lengthways
a few sprigs of fresh thyme
1 tbsp plain flour
150ml white wine
800ml chicken stock
sea salt
black pepper

1 Put the onion, carrot and thyme in the roasting tin with the meat you are cooking. When the meat is done, remove it from the tin and set it aside to rest.

2 Put the roasting tin, with the onion, carrot and thyme and any cooking juices, on the hob over a medium heat. Stir in the flour and cook for a couple of minutes, then add the white wine. Cook until the wine has reduced by half, then pour in the stock and bring to the boil. Continue cooking until the gravy thickens, then season and add any juices from the resting meat. Pass through a sieve and serve in a warm jug.

DIPPING SAUCE SERVES 4

1 tbsp sugar
4 tbsp soy sauce
2 tbsp dry sherry (optional)
1 tsp grated fresh root ginger
1 garlic clove, crushed
juice of 1 lime
1/2 red chilli, finely diced
1 tbsp finely sliced chives

1 Simply place all the ingredients in a small jar, screw on the lid and shake for 10 seconds. Great with cod and crab bonbons.

TZATZIKI SERVES 4

150g Greek yoghurt
½ cucumber, peeled,
   deseeded and diced
2 tbsp chopped fresh mint
½ garlic clove, crushed
small pinch of sugar
sea salt
black pepper

1 Combine all the ingredients, except the salt and pepper, in a bowl. Mix well and leave to stand for 10 minutes so that the flavours can develop before serving. Season to taste.

MAYONNAISE SERVES 4

2 egg yolks
1 tsp Dijon mustard
1 tsp white wine vinegar
250ml groundnut oil
sea salt
black pepper

1 Place your mixing bowl on a tea towel to help keep it steady as you whisk. Put the egg yolks in the bowl – save the whites for another dish or freeze them.

2 Add the mustard and wine vinegar to the egg yolks, then start whisking while adding the oil a drop or so at a time. Continue whisking and slowly adding the oil until you've used it all and the mixture has emulsified to the desired consistency. Season with salt and pepper.

3 For a flavour twist, try adding some garlic, lime juice, harissa or wasabi paste.

INDEX

Thank you everyone

The realization of this book is a massive milestone for me. Eight years ago I was digging up roads and living out my food dreams at home by cooking for my family and friends. Now I've published my own cookbook. It's unbelievable, but it would not have been possible without the help and support of a huge number of special people. Here goes and please forgive me if I miss anyone out.

My wife Lou – without your love and support, nothing I have achieved in my career would have been possible. You made me believe that I could realize my dreams. Your talent to inspire others is one of your finest qualities so never underestimate the impact you have on people's lives. You are an amazing person. Love you always.

My daughter Indie-Roux, for being the light of my life and my constant inspiration to cook family food, and for generally being amazing. You make me smile every single day.

My parents, for their constant love and support and for exposing me to home-cooked food throughout my childhood. I feel so fortunate to have had the upbringing I've had.

My bro Wesley and numerous sisters – Steph, Amber, Georgia and Lauryn. Cheers for being my guinea pigs along with Charlie and Kelly. But Wes – you need to stop moaning that I don't cook for you enough!

My very large and amazing family. You are too many to mention but you know who you are.

Very special thanks to Andy, Kid and Gumbo for their constant support over the years and being so patient while I've been trying to follow my dreams. You are legends!

Jan, Borra and the team at DML for giving me the opportunity to live my dreams and believing in me.

And thank you to everyone at Transworld for helping me to realize my book; ace photographer Martin Poole; Smith & Gilmour for their slick design; Aya Nishimura and Xenia von Oswald for their creative vision for the book; Jinny Johnson for translating from Bristolian into English and making me sound proper intelligent, ha ha. You have all been amazing and far, far exceeded my expectations.

Finally, I'd like to dedicate this book to my cousin Emma G who was taken from us far too early, I know you would have been so proud of me. Love you always.

SOUND MAGIC!

Imagine what it's like in outer space where there is no sound at all! This is because sound needs to travel through air, or through other substances such as water, or solids like wood. Even though we cannot see sound, our ears can tell us where sounds are coming from. But can we always believe our ears? Sound is a natural trickster that can change direction, become quieter or louder, and even make objects move without being touched. Sounds like magic!

BE AN EXPERT MAGICIAN

PREPARING YOUR ROUTINE

There is much more to being a magician than just doing tricks. It is important that you and your assistant practise your whole routine lots of times, so that your performance goes smoothly when you do it for real. You will be a more entertaining magician if you do.

PROPS

Props are all the bit and pieces of equipment that a magician uses during an act. This includes your clothes as well as the tricks themselves. It's a good idea to make a magician's trunk from a large box to keep all your props in. During your routine, you could dip into the trunk, pulling out all sorts of crazy objects (see Distraction). You could also tell jokes about these objects.

PROPS LIST
Magic wand
Top hat
Waistcoat
Silk scarves
Balloons
Paint
Boxes
Plastic tubing
Glass jars
Playing cards

Wine glasses
Tape recorder with headphones
Small radio
Music box mechanism
String
Containers

Coloured paper
Cardboard

SCIENCE
MAGIC
WITH SOUND

CHRIS OXLADE

GLOUCESTER PRESS
LONDON • NEW YORK • SYDNEY

Design
David West Children's Book Design
Designer
Steve Woosnam-Savage
Editor
Suzanne Melia
Illustrator
Ian Thompson
Photographer
Roger Vlitos

© Aladdin Books Ltd 1993
Created and designed by
N.W. Books
28 Percy Street
London W1P 9FF

First published in
Great Britain in 1993 by
Franklin Watts Ltd
96 Leonard Street
London EC2A 4RH

ISBN 0 7496 1340 8

A CIP catalogue record for this book
is available from the British Library

CONTENTS

WHICH TRICKS?

Work out which tricks you want to put in your routine. Put in some long tricks and some short tricks. This will keep your audience interested. If you can, include a trick that you can keep going back to during the routine. Magicians call this a "running gag".

MAGICIAN'S PATTER

Patter is what you say during your routine. Good patter makes a routine much more interesting and allows it to run much more smoothly. It is a good way to entertain your audience during

the slower parts of your routine. Try to make up a story for each trick. Remember to introduce yourself and your assistant at the start and to thank the audience at the end. Practise your patter when you practise your tricks.

DISTRACTION

Distraction is an important part of a magician's routine. By waving a colourful scarf in the air or telling a joke, you can take an audience's attention away from something you'd rather they didn't see!

KEEP IT SECRET

The best magicians never give away their secrets. If anyone asks how your tricks work, just reply "By magic!" Then you can impress people with your tricks again and again.

INTRODUCING MAGIC MELISSA
AND THE
VACUUM JAR TRICK

How is it possible? Magic Melissa silences music simply by sucking up through the tube!

Lower your music box mechanism into the jar, making sure that it does not touch the sides. Now stretch the balloon over the top of the jar to seal the opening. The audience will still be able to hear the music. Now suck as much air as you can from the jar. Squeeze the neck of the balloon between sucks to keep the vacuum. The sound will gradually get quieter.

WHAT YOU NEED
*Music box mechanism
(or a small radio)
Large glass jar
String
Balloons
Plastic tubing*

THE SCIENCE
BEHIND THE TRICK

When you speak, you make the tiny particles (called molecules) which make up air vibrate. The vibrations are passed from one molecule to the next, spreading the sound. Your ear detects the vibrating air so that you can hear sound. But in a vacuum, there is no air, so sound cannot travel. When you first put the music box mechanism into the jar, the sound can travel through the air inside. But when you suck, there is less air. The sound cannot travel so well, so it sounds quieter.

Air leaves the jar

Air is sucked out of the bottle through the tube

1 Cut a circle of card to fit exactly over the top of your glass jar. Cut a small hole in its centre just large enough for the plastic tubing to fit through.

2 Pierce two holes in the card disc and attach the music box mechanism.

3 Cut off the bottom from a balloon and push the neck over a length of plastic tubing. Place in the jar and seal the top with the balloon.

INTRODUCING MAGIC MOLLY
AND THE
MAGIC GLASSES

Magic Molly makes a glass sing and the playing card moves mysteriously.

Put the two wine glasses (with the water already in them) on the table, about 5 cm apart. Ask a volunteer to pick a card from the pack. Put the remaining cards under the edge of one of the glasses and rest the selected card on top of the tilted glass. Now wet your finger in the other glass and run it around the rim. The glass will sing and the card will begin to move!

WHAT YOU NEED
Wine glasses
Playing cards
Water

THE SCIENCE
BEHIND THE TRICK

Running you finger around the glass makes it vibrate. This makes a ringing sound. The pitch of the sound (the note it makes) depends on the level of water in the glass. When the sound reaches the other glass, it also vibrates. Because the level of the water is the same, the glass picks up the vibrations well. This is called *resonance*. The vibrations make the card slide.

Sound waves travel through the air

When the sound waves reach the second glass, it also vibrates

As the glass is rubbed it vibrates, producing sound waves

1 This is a very easy trick to prepare! First of all, find a pack of playing cards and two identical wine glasses.

2 Before you perform your routine, fill both wine glasses to about half full. Make sure that the level of water in both is the same.

INTRODUCING MAGIC MOLLY
AND THE
HEARING HAT TRICK

The amazing hearing hat brings music to Magic Molly's ears!

Make sure that you are wearing the hearing hat before you start the trick. Ask a volunteer from the audience to secretly select one of the tapes, put it into the cassette player and press the PLAY button. Nobody will be able to hear the music. Take off your hat, put it over the headphones, listen, and then tell the audience which tape is being played!

WHAT YOU NEED
Tape recorder with headphones
Thin coloured card
Plastic tubing
Glue

THE SCIENCE
BEHIND THE TRICK

The sound that comes out of the small speakers in the headphones is very quiet. It spreads out from the headphones and only a tiny bit reaches your ears. When you put the hat over the headphones, you can hear the music better. The sound which you would not normally hear is collected in the hat and bounces around or *reverberates* inside the cone.

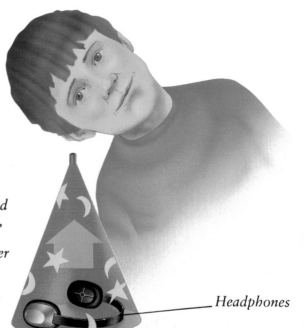

Sound waves are concentrated by the cone, making the sound louder by the time it reaches the top

Headphones

2 Cut off the tip of the cone and glue in a short piece of plastic tubing. Decorate the cone with magic symbols to complete the hat.

1 Roll up a large sheet of card to make a cone shape and trim around the bottom.

INTRODUCING MAGIC MONA
AND THE
TALKING PUPPET

The puppet comes to life as Magic Mona conjures up a voice all of its own.

Have the curtain and tube set up before you start the trick. Your assistant sneaks behind the curtain to operate the glove puppet. Now you can have a conversation with the puppet — and the puppet will talk in your voice! Each time you want the puppet to speak, talk into the end of the tube. You can disguise the tube by covering the end with a silk scarf, and pretending to talk into it. This is an opportunity for some good patter.

WHAT YOU NEED
Cardboard tubes
Balloons
Plastic tubing
Thin card
Silk scarf
Glove puppet
Sticky tape

THE SCIENCE
BEHIND THE TRICK

When an object makes a sound, it makes the air around it vibrate. The vibrations (or waves) spread out in all directions. Our ears detect the sound and the direction from which it is coming. When you speak into the tube, the sound waves cannot spread out. They bounce down the tube and come out of the cone at the end. Your voice seems to come from the puppet.

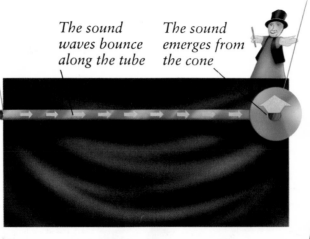

The sound waves bounce along the tube

The sound emerges from the cone

GETTING
PREPARED

1 Join cardboard tubes together to make a long tube. Using a balloon, attach a piece of plastic tubing to one end.

3 Hang a large cloth across your stage as shown and hang the tube behind it.

2 On the other end of the tube, attach a cone made from card.

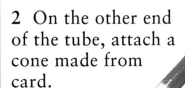

INTRODUCING MAGIC MIRANDA
AND THE
PICK THE CARD TRICK

Magic Miranda stuns her audience by guessing the card correctly every time!

Ask your assistant to tie the blindfold around your head, and sit down at the table. Now ask a volunteer to point at one of the cards on the board. Pretend to concentrate hard, laying your head on the table. Your assistant now secretly scratches the table the correct number of times, indicating which card has been chosen. Call out the card!

WHAT YOU NEED
Playing cards
Coloured card
Sticky putty

THE SCIENCE BEHIND THE TRICK

We normally think of sound travelling through the air. However, it also travels through liquids and solids too. In fact, sound travels much better in liquids and solids than it does in the air. The scratching is too quiet for its sound to be heard through the air by the audience, but you can hear it easily through the solid wood of the table.

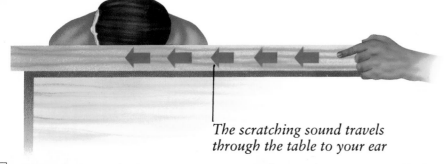

The scratching sound travels through the table to your ear

16

1 Take ten cards from a pack of playing cards (ace, two, three, etc.). Using sticky putty, attach the cards to a piece of card in two rows of five.

2 You will also need a blindfold. You can make this from a coloured silk scarf. Make sure the audience know you can't see the cards.

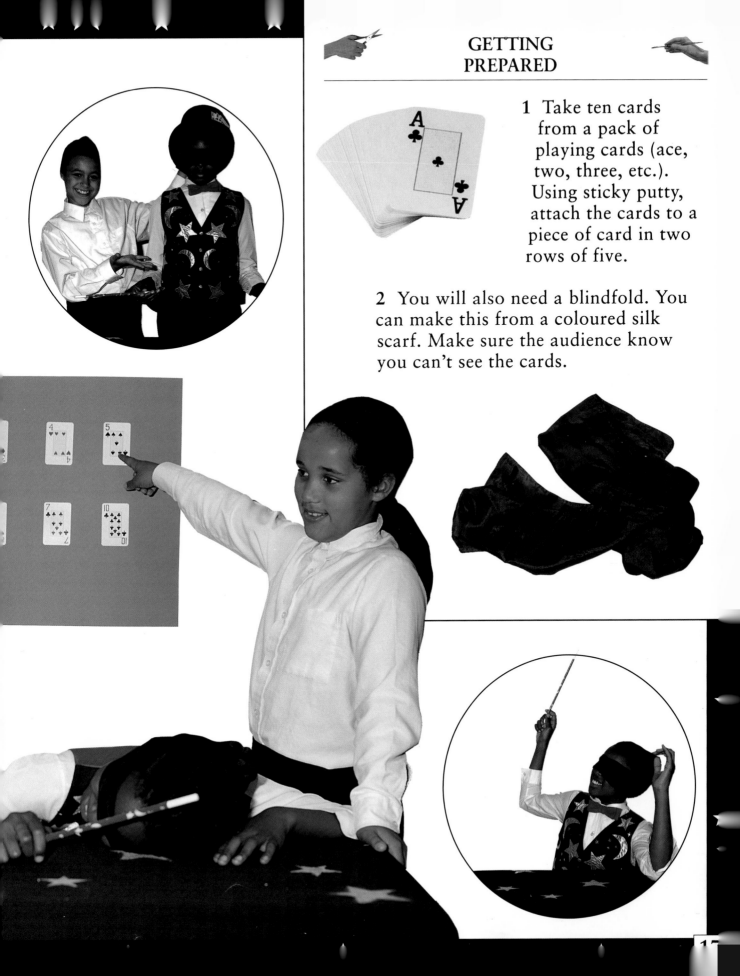

INTRODUCING MAGIC MOLLY
AND THE
TELEPORTING TRICK

Magic Molly transports her assistant from one side of the stage to the other.

Hang two curtains at the back of your stage. Now send your assistant behind the left curtain and talk to him or her so that the audience can hear a voice. Now announce that you have transported your assistant to behind the other curtain. Talk to them again. This time your assistant's voice appears to be behind the other curtain – teleported!

WHAT YOU NEED
Yoghurt pots
Cardboard box
String
Coloured paper
Egg boxes or trays
Glue
Paints

THE SCIENCE
BEHIND THE TRICK

When your assistant speaks into the yoghurt pot of the string telephone, their voice makes the bottom of the pot vibrate. These vibrations travel along the string and come out of the cone at the other end. The egg boxes in the box absorb your assistant's voice.

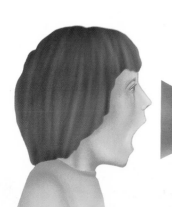

The vibrations caused by the sound of a voice travel down the string and emerge at the other end

1 Find a large cardboard box, and cut off or fold down the flaps. Decorate the outside of the box with magic symbols. Line the inside of the box with egg boxes or egg trays.

2 Thread a long string through a yoghurt and tie a knot inside. Pierce a hole in the bottom of the box, push the loose end of the string through and add a second pot. Add a paper cone.

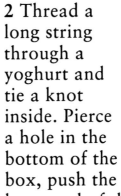

INTRODUCING MAGIC MOLLY
AND THE
FIND THE BALL TRICK

Which jar is the ball in? Magic Molly can tell by tapping with her magic wand!

Arrange the three jars in a row on the table and remove the lids. Now ask for a volunteer. With your back turned, ask them to put the ball into one of the jars and then put on all the lids. Now tap each jar in turn (to disguise the ringing sounds you could say "Is it here ... or here ... or here?" as you tap). The jar with the odd note is where the ball is.

WHAT YOU NEED
Glass jars with lids
Ball
Water

THE SCIENCE BEHIND THE TRICK

When you strike a jar with your wand, it makes a ringing sound. The pitch of the sound (the sort of note it makes) depends on the size of the jar and the amount of water in it. (To see the effect, try tapping a jar as you pour water into it — the note will gradually get higher.) When the ball is put into a jar, it makes the water level rise, changing the note.

The ball changes the level of the water

1 Collect together three identical glass jars. The jars need to be large enough for the ball to fit into. Paint all the jars with oil-based paint so that you can't see through the glass.

2 Fill each jar half-full of water. The level of water in each one must be the same (you could make sure that you put the same amount of water in each jar by filling them from a measuring cup). Finally, find a ball which will sink in water.

WHAT YOU NEED
Two cardboard boxes
Egg boxes or trays
Small radio
Tissue paper
Cloths
Coloured paper
Sticky tape
Glue

INTRODUCING MAGIC MAX
AND THE
WHISPERING BOX

The box is empty – so where are the strange whispering sounds coming from?

Start by showing the smaller box to the audience so that they can see that it is empty. Ask for a volunteer to come forward and listen to the box – there will be silence, of course! Now put the smaller box on top of the larger box. Ask your volunteer to listen again by putting an ear against the box. There will be a quiet whispering from inside!

THE SCIENCE
BEHIND THE TRICK

The packing of egg boxes, tissue paper and cloth absorbs the sound coming from the radio. (Sound-proof rooms often have egg-box like walls.) Some sound travels up the tube and makes the smaller box vibrate. So the radio can be heard when you put your ear to the box.

Sound waves travel up the tube and are amplified by the smaller box

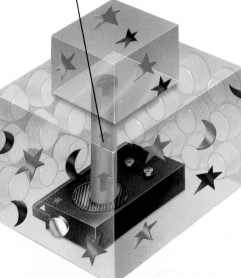

22

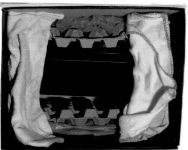

1 Put the radio inside the larger box with the speaker pointing upwards. Pack egg boxes, tissue paper and cloth around it, but don't cover the speaker.

2 Cut a rectangle of card to fit inside the larger box, and make a card tube to go through the middle of the rectangle as shown.

3 Put the rectangle into the box so that the bottom of the tube touches the speaker. Cut a hole in the box for the tube to poke through.

INTRODUCING MAGIC MELISSA
AND THE
AMPLIFYING BOX TRICK

Magic Melissa turns up the volume without ever touching the radio dial!

Put the radio on the table, turn it on and adjust the volume so that the sound is quite quiet. Now announce that you can make the sound louder or softer without touching the radio. Put the box in front of the radio, first with the big hole next to it, then with the small hole next to it. The sound will get louder and then quieter!

WHAT YOU NEED
Cardboard box
Thin card
Tissue paper
Small radio
Sticky tape
Glue

THE SCIENCE BEHIND THE TRICK

When the box is not in front of the radio, the sound from the speaker spreads out. The audience sitting in front of the radio only hear a small amount of the sound. With the box in front, the cone collects the sound and sends it all towards the audience. This makes the radio sound louder as it amplifies the sound.

The sound is gathered together and directed towards the audience

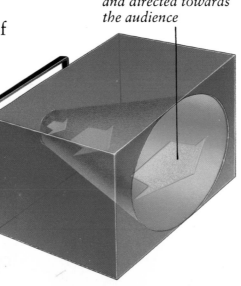

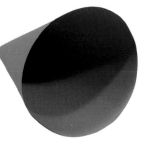

2 Cut two holes (one large and one small) in opposite sides of the box. Cover the box with tissue paper to hide the holes.

3 Stick the cone inside over the holes.

1 Using thin card, make a cone to fit inside the box. Snip off the top to make a hole at the narrow end.

INTRODUCING MAGIC MERVYN
AND THE
DISAPPEARING WATER

It doesn't matter which of Magic Mervyn's bottles the audience choose, it's always empty!

Before you start the trick, attach the small bottle of water to your right arm with some sticky tape. Now ask someone to predict which of the bottles on the table has water in it. Shake the bottle with your left hand — it will sound empty. Pick up the other bottle with your right hand and shake it — it will sound full!

WHAT YOU NEED
A small bottle
Two medium-sized bottles
Oil-based paint
Water

THE SCIENCE BEHIND THE TRICK

Our ears are very good at picking up sound, and can work out approximately where sound is coming from — but not exactly. When you shake the empty bottle in your right hand, the water in the bottle up your sleeve makes a sloshing noise. Because the noise comes from almost where the members of the audience expect it to, they do not suspect anything.

Bottle of water is hidden on the right arm

1 Find two identical medium-sized bottles. Clean them and remove any labels. Paint them with oil-based paint so that you cannot see inside and put on their lids.

2 Find a small bottle which you can hide up your sleeve without it looking too obvious. Half fill it with water and screw on the top.

HINTS AND TIPS

Here are some hints and tips for making your props. Good props will make your act look more professional. So spend time making and decorating your props, and look after them carefully. As well as the special props you need for each trick, try to make some general props such as a waistcoat and magic wand.

Decorate your props with magic shapes cut from coloured paper. Paint bottles and tubes with oil-based paint.

You will need sticky-tape and glue to make props. Double-sided tape might also be useful. You can use sticky putty or special plastic sealant to make water-proof joints.

Try cutting magic shapes out of card and using the holes to make stencils.

Your act will look extra professional if you make a proper stage set. This is easy if you have a backcloth to hang behind the stage. A large piece of black cloth would be most effective. Use silver paint to create stars and moons. Decorate pieces of cloth to throw over your table. The overall effect should be a set that creates an atmosphere of mystery and magic.

Make your own magician's clothes. Try to find an old hat and waistcoat to decorate. If you can find some silvery material, cut out stars and moons and sew them on. An alternative is sequins. Use anything that is shiney and dramatic so you look professional.

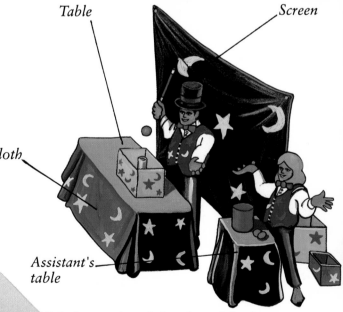

Table *Screen*

Cloth

Assistant's table

Make a magician's table by draping a cloth over a table. You can put the props underneath out of

GLOSSARY

AMPLIFY To make sound louder using a sound box or cone.

MOLECULES The tiny particles of which substances are made.

PITCH The highness or lowness of a sound. It depends on the frequency of the vibration causing the sound.

RESONANCE When a sound makes another object produce a sound because it has the same natural frequency of vibration.

REVERBERATION The bouncing of sound waves within a small space.

SOUND WAVES A regular pattern of changes in the pressure of molecules in solids, liquids or gases, such as air.

SOUNDPROOFING Materials that muffle sound by bouncing it in all directions. A room or box can be soundproofed.

VIBRATION A rapid movement back and forth, causing a sound.

INDEX